MW01615633

KAREN CURRY PARKER

INTRODUCTION
TO
QUANTUM
HUMAN DESIGN™

3RD EDITION

The highest expression of humankind is the full engagement and joy that allows us to evolve by learning from and leaving the past behind, by consciously and consistently expressing our authentic potential and making our unique contribution to the world, taking our direction from Spirit, being physically vital, having all the resources we need to fulfill our destiny and taking actions that are only for the greater good of the world. In other words, we're designed to feel good being who we are and doing what we came here to do.

- Karen Curry Parker

HUMANDESIGN
— PRESS —

An Imprint for GracePoint Publishing (www.GracePointPublishing.com)

GracePoint Matrix, LLC
624 S. Cascade Ave
Suite 201
Colorado Springs, CO 80903
www.GracePointMatrix.com
Email: Admin@GracePointMatrix.com
SAN # 991-6032

First Edition published in 2020; Second Edition published in 2020

LCCN: 2020950175 3rd Edition

ISBN: (Paperback) 978-0-9893336-9-6
eISBN: 978-0-9992517-0-6

Books may be purchased for educational, business, or sales promotional use. For bulk order requests and price schedule contact:
Orders@GracePointPublishing.com

Learn more about Quantum Human Design on the website.

quantumhumandesign.com

Other Books and Resources by Karen Curry Parker

Abundance by Design

Human Design Workbook

Inside the Body of God

Introduction to Quantum Human Design™ 2nd Edition

Quantum Human Design™ Activation Cards

*Quantum Human Design™ Activation Cards
Companion Book*

QHD Quantum Activation Card Deck (iPhone App)

Human Design and the Coronavirus

*The Quantum Human: The Evolution of Consciousness and the
Solar Plexus Mutation in Human Design*

Understanding Human Design

Quantum Human Design™ Evolution Guide 2023

Contents

What Is
Quantum Human Design?

Quantum Human Design is often called the "new astrology," and the "intersection of science and spirituality." Your Quantum Human Design chart is formulated by taking your birth date, time, and location—giving you specific information about your life path, style of working, relationship blueprint, how you experience energy in the world, and most importantly, how to create a truly meaningful and authentic life.

Quantum Human Design is a synthesis of Eastern and Western astrology, the Chinese I Ching, the Judaic Kabbalah, the Hindu chakra system and quantum physics.

If you're like most of our clients, you've probably attended multiple personal growth seminars and read lots of books about manifesting change and creating success in your life. Maybe you've even studied specific techniques to help you release blocks and get yourself unstuck.

But even though you've been doing everything right, you still haven't seen the results you've been hoping for. It's not your fault.

The single most important reason you may have not had the success you've been working so hard for is this:

A *one-size-fits-all* approach to life does not work.

All people are equally valuable and important, and each of us has our own energetic blueprint and individual style of operating successfully in life. What might work for one person doesn't necessarily work for another.

A Human Design chart offers an astonishingly accurate guide to your personality, as well as direction and guidance on how you can deal with challenges in your life. It also shows you your personal "formula" for creating what you want in your life.

Human Design charts have been notoriously difficult to interpret and decipher—until now. **Quantum Human Design, a modern way of interpreting Human Design, offers an incredibly down-to-earth, practical way to understand your Human Design chart.**

Quantum Human Design **specialists** are highly trained coaches, mentors, and guides who have learned a way of interpreting your chart that is simple, easy to follow, clear, and gives you solid, workable strategies to help you discover exactly what you need to do to bring out the best of who you are in your life.

Learning your Human Design:

- Confirms what you already know, sense, or have felt about yourself.
- Gives you full permission and confidence to really step fully into your truth.

- Confirms the themes you may have noticed playing out in your life and relationships.
- Gives you a deeper understanding as to why you are the way you are and feel the way you do.
- Enables you to not take things personally because you realize everything is just energy.
- Deepens compassion, patience. and ultimately love for yourself and others.

Think of it this way:

Human Design is a synthesis of ancient wisdom and modern science. It is a collection of all the potential archetypes located in a single map. That map not only tells you where you would feel better and helps you navigate a path to get there, but it also gives you a new way of thinking about who you really are.

Quantum Human Design teaches you to look at your Human Design chart (your personal map) as a story. Over the course of your life, you've been told a *story* of who you are. Maybe that story led down a career path that isn't really making your soul soar. Maybe your story has you living out patterns that keep you from believing you can have what you really want in your life. Maybe the story you've been trying to keep up with throughout life isn't even really *your* story.

Quantum Human Design will give you the words—the story— of who you truly are.

If you're going to create an authentic life—a life that is yours— you must begin with knowing who you are and what you need to do to get started living the story you were born to live.

Your personal Quantum Human Design chart can reveal your strengths, your weaknesses, and, perhaps most importantly, your potential. Prepare for repetitive difficulties that you might encounter throughout your life and embrace the opportunity to grow as you understand your personal Human Design Strategy.

You'll discover your path to living an aligned, authentic, vital, and truly meaningful life simply by following the directions set out in your Human Design chart—the owner's manual to your life.

The Human Design Chart

Design

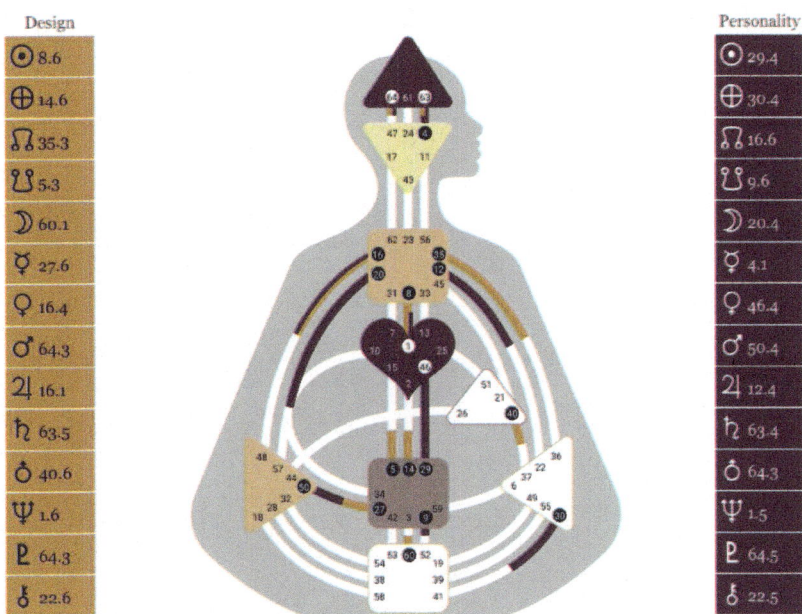

Personality

Your Human Design is the key to understanding your energy, your life purpose, your life path, and your soul's journey in this lifetime. You are a once-in-a-lifetime cosmic event and the fulfillment of your potential and purpose is the greatest gift you can give the world. —Karen Curry Parker

Get your free Quantum Human Design Chart
freehumandesignchart.com

Your Quantum Blueprint

The moment of your conception marks an important, once-in-a-lifetime event. At that moment the Universe joined your soul with a powerful story, the story of your life. The story of *you* is so unique that it has never been on the planet before and will never be on the planet again.

Over the course of your life, you may have forgotten your story. You may have been told that you should be a certain way or act a certain way and that there are key formulas you have to follow to be successful or healthy.

If you're like most people, you may have struggled to make the rules you were given fit and work for you. You may have followed the rules very well and still not gotten the results for which you were hoping. Your journey may have left you feeling depleted and not good enough. You may have lost touch with the powerful story of who you truly are and felt that there is something wrong with you.

There is nothing wrong with you, you just need to remember who you truly are.

It makes sense that if you are a once-in-a-lifetime event in this Universe that there are no formulas for health and vitality, abundance, right relationship, right work, or success in life other than the ones that work for you.

There is no one-size-fits-all approach to creating success. In fact, even the definition of success is unique to each one of us. The greatest source of pain in life is the disconnect from our *authentic self*—the real story of who you truly are.

When we try to squeeze the powerful essence of who we are behind masks or into small definitions of who we should be, it unleashes a subtle restlessness inside of us. This subtle restlessness creates stress and unhappiness, an inner awareness that you're not living your life purpose or being true to yourself and a sense that there's more to the story.

YOUR ROADMAP TO REMEMBER WHY YOU ARE HERE

WHEN YOU GET LOST IN YOUR HUMAN SUIT, ALLOW YOUR BODY CHART TO BE YOUR BEACON BACK HOME.

This basic introduction is designed to jog your memory, to push against that inner restlessness that you may feel, and to help you answer the most important questions in the world: Who are you? And why are you here?

In this book, you'll learn the pieces separately, but the true magic or brilliance is when you learn to put them all back together into a fully synthesized story. May these words begin the start of your journey back to remembering the truth of what you came here to experience, what you came here to do, and who you came here to be!

Human Design Shows Us the Nexus Between the Human and Spiritual Experience

Your Human Design chart is made of two distinctly different aspects: your *soul purpose* and your *life purpose*. The purpose of life is growth and expansion. Our souls manifest on Earth to experience whatever they need to experience to add to the growth of the Universe.

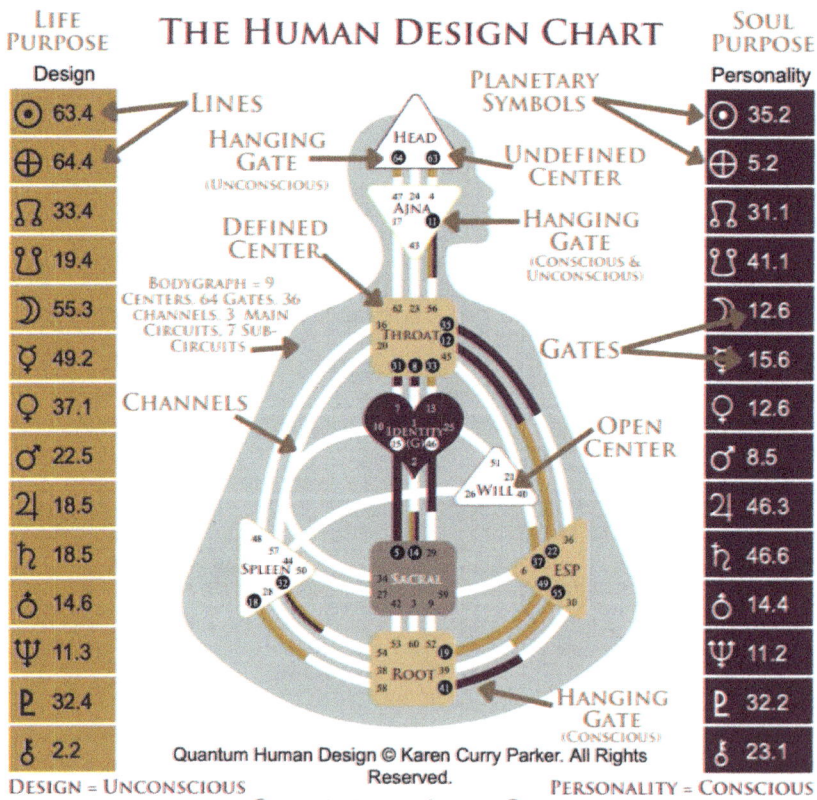

THE HUMAN DESIGN CHART

Quantum Human Design © Karen Curry Parker. All Rights Reserved.

Your life purpose is the story of who you are in this incarnation. This story is encoded in your energy blueprint as well as in your genetic and epigenetic lineage. At the moment of your birth, your soul purpose integrated with your life purpose to create a once-in-a-lifetime event that is YOU!

Over the course of our lives, we often experience a struggle between elements of our soul purpose and our life purpose. These inner struggles are often "pre-scripted" into the story of our lives. Many people find that when they really understand their Human Design, they gain a deeper understanding of their own struggles. This awareness helps us gain new levels of self-mastery so that we can fulfill our potential in a richer, more meaningful way.

The Human Design chart is a visual representation of the sum of human possibilities and energies.

The entire collection of archetypes of humanity is contained within the structural framework of the chart. All the possibilities for the expression of being human appear here.

The chart shows us the different ways we love, lead, learn, know, grow, sense, and so much more. Your chart shows you your best strategy for making money, having great relationships, being healthy, and staying creatively fulfilled.

Your unique chart helps you understand how you work and how to best make your life work for you. Each individual chart is a map of how you process energy.

Your chart reveals your strengths, your potential weaknesses, your gifts, and your talents. Most importantly, it tells the story of who you are, why you are here, and how you can live a life that is in alignment with the truth of who you really are.

Each individual chart is calculated using your birth date, time, and place.

- The geometric shapes represent the nine centers.
- The lines represent the channels.
- The numbers represent the gates.
- The colors reveal your strengths, potential weaknesses, gifts, and talents.

If you look closely at the chart, you might see some visual evidence of the influencing wisdom behind Human Design. For example, the geometric shapes called *centers* look very similar to the seven chakras.

"YOU ARE AN INFINITE POWERFUL CREATOR, LIVING IN A HUMAN STORY."

KAREN CURRY PARKER

If you turn the chart upside down, it looks very similar to the Kabbalah Tree of Life.

Or you may notice that sixty-four numbers appear on the chart. These numbers, called gates, correlate to the sixty-four hexagrams from the Chinese I Ching. In the I Ching, a hexagram is a figure composed of six stacked horizontal lines, where each line is either yang (a solid line) or yin (a line with a gap in the center).

TRANSPERSONAL LINES ARE ENERGIES THAT ARE ALL ABOUT EXPERIENCES IN RELATIONSHIPS WITH OTHERS.

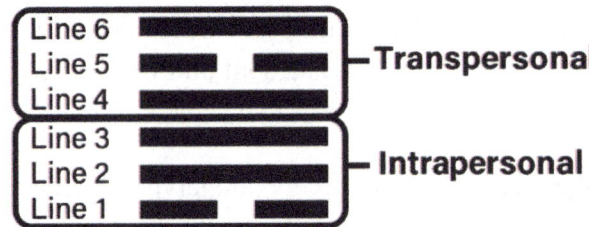

INTRAPERSONAL LINES ARE ENERGIES THAT ARE SELF-FOCUSED AND ALL ABOUT PERSONAL EXPERIENCE AND UNDERSTANDING.

@KarenCurryParker

Though you can see pieces of these ancient wisdom teachings in the chart, Human Design is something new and unique, a new tool to help people in a brand-new way.

It is important to realize that when you look at parts of the chart, they are simply pieces. To make learning about Human Design easier, we have to start first by taking the chart apart and covering each piece one by one.

But once you have a handle on how the chart is constructed, and how to read it, the story—or personal energy map—is revealed when you put all of the pieces together.

The story of each chart is based on the synthesis of everything within the chart. Each one is different and unique. It's in the sum all the parts of the chart that your personal energy map is revealed.

Human Design involves a lot of data and that's why we break it down into bite-size, digestible pieces, but understand that by doing so we are taking these pieces out of context. It's when we put them back together and look at the whole picture, the entire Design in its wholeness, we see the story of the beauty, magnificence, and one-of-a-kind magic that you are!

We've been given a great gift, an invaluable insight into what it means to embody this form as a soul and live out a specific life story.

This blueprint shows us every archetypal theme of what it means to be a human being. It shows us our potential, provides answers to our longing questions, and gives us full permission to step into our truth, allowing us to live a life unmasked in realness and the unapologetically authentic expressions of our divine essence and innate nature.

It's so easy to stay hidden, live small, and believe we are what we are not, but living in that misalignment literally sucks the life and energy from you and manifests itself as pain. You can only deny your truth for so long.

The world needs you—all of you—-to be healed and whole, living in alignment with the fullness of your power, fulfilling your purpose of being who you are. That is your gift, your purpose, and your contribution to the collective.

• We ALL Have ALL of the Chart •

Everything in a Human Design chart represents an archetypal energy that you can express in an infinite number of ways.

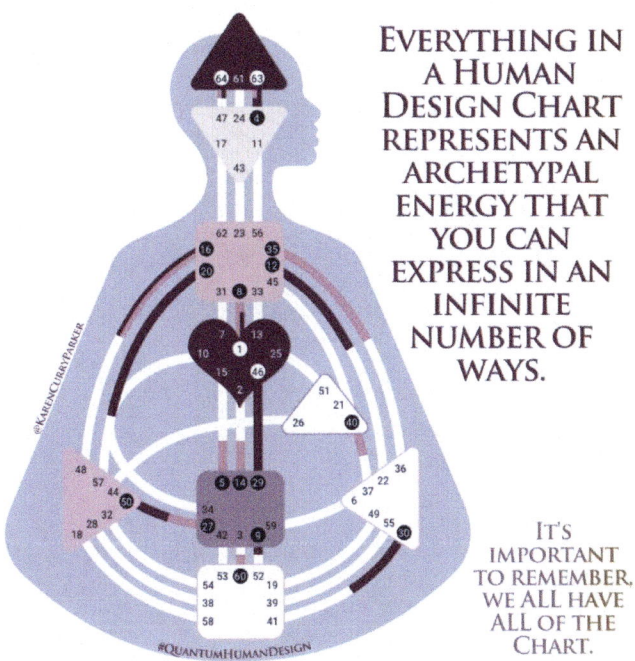

EVERYTHING IN A HUMAN DESIGN CHART REPRESENTS AN ARCHETYPAL ENERGY THAT YOU CAN EXPRESS IN AN INFINITE NUMBER OF WAYS.

IT'S IMPORTANT TO REMEMBER, WE ALL HAVE ALL OF THE CHART.

The expression of each element of your chart is operating on a spectrum; it has a high end, a low end, and the space in between.

It's important to remember we all have ALL of the chart. We can experience all of the energies in the Human Design chart in the high or low expression of the circuitry that's defined in our specific chart. We experience our definition more consistently than our openness.

We're here to support you in consciously expressing the highest possible potential of your unique energy, the defined themes of your channels and gates.

*Please note, by no means does this book represent the whole picture about you and your unique Design no more than one chromosome would represent your whole biology. You're a magnificent multidimensional being with great depth and complexity. This is just an introduction to understanding the Quantum Human Design basics, or scratching the surface, at best.

Why the New Language?

Words create; they endure. They allow for unity. They transmit. They are the interface between the Divine and the Human. Words are power. They translate the infinite to the finite. Words are a code for a story. Words carry frequencies of energy, and our DNA responds to that language.

When Ra Uru Hu, the founder of Human Design, first shared his transmission of the system, he did so in a way that penetrated and shocked people into waking up. He needed to speak into the "not-self" or the inauthentic self, in order to quickly get people's attention and it worked.

Having personally known and worked with Ra and after having studied and taught Human Design for over two decades, I have been divinely inspired to continue what Ra started. When he died of a heart attack in 2011, it's as if the language of Human Design was locked, stuck in the context of the not-self of the late eighties and also to his death. I share now the flip side of this beautiful tool and speak to the knowledge imparted through Ra, but with an empowering and higher vibrational frequency language that I call Quantum Human Design.

Quantum Human Design is a new and transformed Human Design language that is more expansive, empowering, and expressive, and it comes with a more comprehensive understanding. I have deliberately engineered and upgraded the Human Design vocabulary to a powerful, positive, higher vibrational frequency of energy to help you fully activate your potential.

Quantum Human Design will provide you with a new way to see your Human Design chart and tell a bigger and better story about what's possible for you!

Type, Strategy, and Emotional Theme

Here are the five Energy Types in Quantum Human Design (with the traditional Human Design name in parentheses) and their decision-making Strategy.

1. **Initiator** (Manifestor)—inform then initiate.

2. **Orchestrator** (Projector)—wait for recognition and invitation.

3. **Alchemist** (Generator)—wait to respond.

4. **Time Bender** (Manifesting Generator)—wait to respond, envision, inform, then take action.

5. **Calibrator** (Reflector)—wait a Lunar cycle.

Your Human Design Type shows you exactly how to create and live in a way that is most empowering, fulfilling, dynamic, and successful.

Your Type is the hardwiring of your energetic configuration and your unique way of interacting with the world. Each Type has a unique decision-making Strategy. Knowing your Type and Strategy can help you develop the confidence and trust in your capacity and ability to make reliable and correct decisions for yourself.

Each Type has a different role and different way of interacting with others and the world.

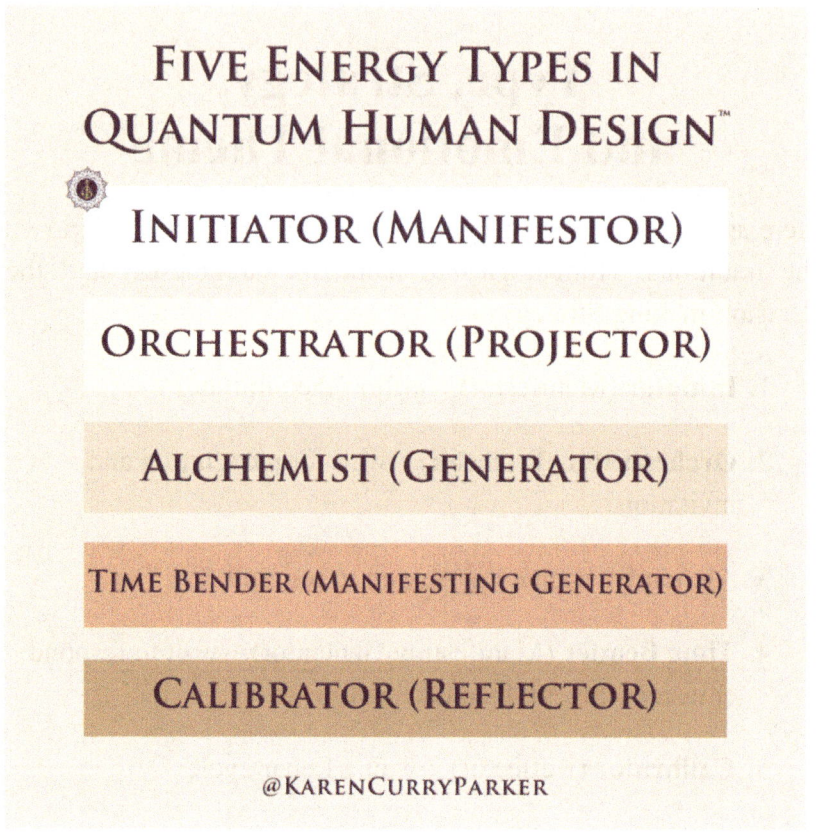

FIVE ENERGY TYPES IN QUANTUM HUMAN DESIGN™

INITIATOR (MANIFESTOR)

ORCHESTRATOR (PROJECTOR)

ALCHEMIST (GENERATOR)

TIME BENDER (MANIFESTING GENERATOR)

CALIBRATOR (REFLECTOR)

@KARENCURRYPARKER

Most of us aren't raised to really live out the full power and potential of who we are. We are all powerful creators, but in order to use our power in the most efficient and best way, we need to know and understand how we operate.

Every Energy Type in Human Design has a specific Strategy. A Strategy is a unique way of making decisions and taking action in the world.

Strategy is the most important knowledge piece to put into play: practice and experiment with living out in your everyday life.

STRATEGY BY QUANTUM HUMAN DESIGN™ TYPE

QUANTUM HUMAN DESIGN™ (TRADITIONAL)

INITIATOR (MANIFESTOR)	INFORM THEN INITIATE
ORCHESTRATOR (PROJECTOR)	WAIT FOR RECOGNITION & INVITATION
ALCHEMIST (GENERATOR)	WAIT TO RESPOND
TIME BENDER (MANIFESTING GENERATOR)	WAIT TO RESPOND, ENVISION, INFORM THEN TAKE ACTION
CALIBRATOR (REFLECTOR)	WAIT A LUNAR CYCLE

@KARENCURRYPARKER

HTTPS://KARENCURRYPARKER.TEACHABLE.COM

If you're not following your Strategy, it's like trying to build a house and telling the builders to skip pouring the concrete for laying the foundation because you want your house built without it.

Your Strategy is your personal way to make effective decisions in your life, just like laying the correct foundation will allow a sturdy, secure home to be built upon it. These are important key pieces that you choose to commit to or not.

Your Strategy gives you key information about how you operate your human vehicle in the world, how to make the right choices with less resistance, and how to recognize when you are on the right path or out of alignment with your truth. If you want to live out the fullest expression of your unique Design, following your Strategy according to your Type is the way.

Think about it—if we're all different, a one-size-fits-all approach to creating a happy, successful life doesn't make sense. All people are equally valuable and important, but each of us has our own energetic blueprint and individual style of operating successfully in life. What might work for one person won't necessarily work for another.

The struggle to fit in and embrace society's definition of what is "right" and "successful" is really just about energy. The way we feel about ourselves, the rules and values of society, and the way we react to life are all dictated by our own energy field and the bigger collective energy field.

Following your Strategy will help you align more naturally with your life purpose, minimize resistance, and make strong and healthy decisions that feel good and right for you. This will bring more meaning and joy in your life, and you will find that will truly fulfill your personal destiny.

• Emotional Theme •

Each energy Type has an emotional theme, which is simply part of a person's life and brings them lessons as well as opportunities for growth. When you experience your emotional theme in a strong way, it's usually a sign that you are not living true to yourself (in energetic alignment) or you're not following your Strategy. It's always good to take a step back and evaluate your life if you're feeling your emotional theme in a powerful way.

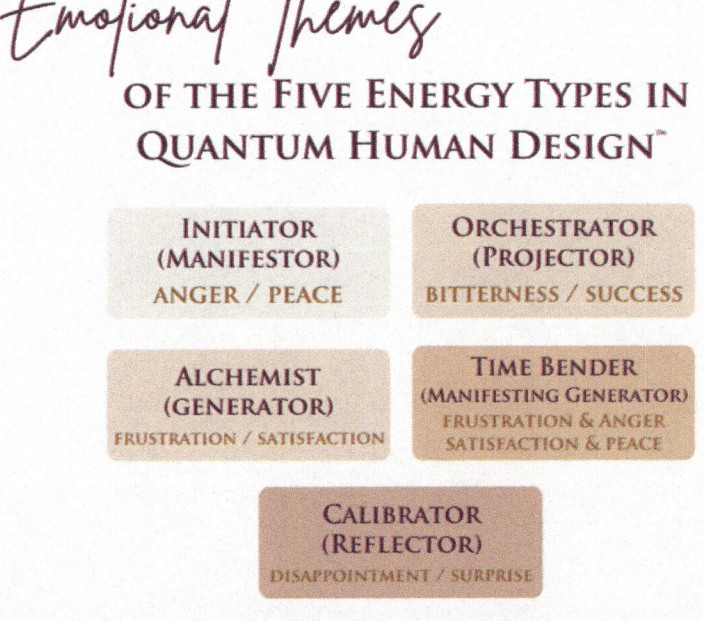

Emotional Themes

OF THE FIVE ENERGY TYPES IN QUANTUM HUMAN DESIGN™

INITIATOR (MANIFESTOR) ANGER / PEACE	**ORCHESTRATOR (PROJECTOR)** BITTERNESS / SUCCESS
ALCHEMIST (GENERATOR) FRUSTRATION / SATISFACTION	**TIME BENDER (MANIFESTING GENERATOR)** FRUSTRATION & ANGER SATISFACTION & PEACE
CALIBRATOR (REFLECTOR) DISAPPOINTMENT / SURPRISE	

@KARENCURRYPARKER

HTTPS://KARENCURRYPARKER.TEACHABLE.COM

When you live your life according to your Strategy, you lessen the intensity of your experience with your emotional theme. Following your Strategy makes your entire life experience easier and more enjoyable.

The emotional theme is thematic, meaning that you will either be experiencing the emotions of your theme yourself or you may be experiencing them in other people around you who are responding to your behavior.

• The Initiator •

Initiator (Manifestor)
9 Percent of the Population

Initiators are the cosmically initiating force on the planet through their connection to the Divine. They are here to get the ball rolling and then move on to the next thing.

Initiators have tremendous initiating power. They can start projects and act independently. Society as a whole has been taught and conditioned to just go out and "do it" or "make it happen," but this type of independent action is exclusive to the Initiator.

Initiators have an open Sacral Center and therefore, they don't have sustainable energy and are not here to work in a traditional way or the same way as the Alchemists (Generators) and Time Benders (Manifesting Generators). Properly channeled Initiator energy gives the other four Types something to respond to.

Many Initiators struggle to learn how to use their power appropriately and may have been conditioned to hide their power or suppress their initiation energy since they were children.

Initiators have an internal, nonverbal creative flow and in order to eliminate the resistance from those around them, they need to inform the people who will be affected by their actions before they act. This simple act of informing builds trust and paves the way for them to move freely and without resistance.

Spiritual Purpose: Translate divine inspiration into action.

Quantum Purpose: To initiate people into the frequency of transformation and creativity through direct access to the quantum pulse and pure inspiration. By being attuned to their authentic creative impulses, the Initiator creates an energetic opening for others to do the same.

Strategy: Inform others before taking action.

Emotional Theme: Anger due to creative flow disruption. They naturally have an internal nonverbal creative flow.

Potential Challenges: Reclaiming and living in their power and being patient when things seem to not be moving fast enough.

• The Alchemist •

Alchemist (Generator)
37 Percent of the Population

Alchemists are the workforce and life-force energy on the planet, the builders and doers of the world.

They're here to become highly skilled in whatever it is they respond to and create. If they're patient and wait to respond to what shows up in their outer reality, instead of trying to figure things out with their mind in regard to what they should be doing, they'll become fully activated in their purpose.

Alchemists may feel frustrated, often because they know they're here to do something that fulfills their full potential and things aren't moving fast enough. They're conditioned by the world to use their thinking and the power of their mind to set their path to self-actualization, but the truth is that their path is revealed to them by the world outside of them!

It takes faith and understanding of how to connect to that path correctly to align themselves with their destiny and ultimate fulfillment of their potential. Alchemists need to wait for things to show up in their outer reality which is a sign and confirmation that it's the right idea to take action on.

Spiritual Purpose: Turn inspiration into form.

Quantum Purpose: To physically manifest creativity and express it through devotion.

Strategy: Wait to respond. Wait for something to show up in their outer reality in order for them to respond.

Emotional Theme: Frustration due to momentum. They may not feel like things are moving fast enough for them. They have a stair-step learning curve and will hit plateaus but when encouraged to not give up or quit completely, they'll eventually have a breakthrough and reach mastery.

Potential Challenge: Endurance and waiting on divine timing.

• The Time Bender •

Time Bender (Manifesting Generator)
33 Percent of the Population

Time Benders are a hybrid of the Initiator (Manifestor) and Alchemist (Generator). They are the workforce, life-force energy, builders, and doers of the world like the Alchemists; however, they also have some traits of the Initiator like the internal nonverbal creative flow and taking action, but *only* after they've followed their Strategy of waiting to respond.

It's correct for the Time Bender to be doing many things at once (multi-tasking) while they are waiting for something to show up in their outer reality for them to respond to.

They move fast and skip steps to find the fastest and most efficient way to the end result. (Sometimes they may have to go back and complete the steps they skipped if they find them to be important.)

They have a deep inner awareness to know what's right for them, a strong intuition turned on by gut-level responses that will place them in the right place at the right time doing the right work and having the right impact.

Spiritual Purpose: Turn inspiration into form.

Quantum Purpose: To physically manifest creativity and speed up the quantum process and linear time. They find places where they can skip steps, creating shortcuts and expediting the process. Shortcuts mean bending time. They shift the way we do things and are able to manifest more than one thing at a time.

Strategy: Wait to respond, envision, inform, then take action.

Emotional Theme: Frustration and anger due to creative flow disruption and momentum. They have an internal nonverbal creative flow like the Initiator (Manifestor). They have a place where they are so intimately connected to Source and the quantum field that they are directly moving through the quantum field. This is possible only in response.

Potential Challenge: Sense of aloneness and disconnection from Spirit and learning how to surrender to time! They can influence time, but they cannot control it. They need to get into alignment with time to minimize the momentum of the energy of frustration. Learn to let go of attachment to time and surrender to universal timing.

• The Orchestrator •

Orchestrator (Projector)
20 Percent of the Population

Orchestrators are the ones who get and sense the necessary information and resources others need. Having an open Sacral Center, they are not here to work in the traditional nine-to-five way, especially if it's physical labor.

They're here to lead, guide, direct, and manage "their people," the ones who see, recognize, value, and invite them. Otherwise they will be losing and leaking energy.

Orchestrators have the energy to guide and direct their people, not do the work themselves. Some believe they can initiate and do more than they're capable of because they're taking in the sacral energy (workforce/life-force energy) of others and amplifying it. But it's not sustainable for them to hold on to this energy, those who do will experience burnout (a lot of Orchestrators experience burnout at forty.)

Orchestrators are also constantly taking in the energy of the entire planet Earth in their energy field. Even if they're sitting on the couch watching Netflix, they're clearing and transmuting all of the hurting on the planet and creating a new template. They're moving things on the ethereal plane.

Spiritual Purpose: To anchor the energetic template of what we are here to create; to align the energy of the world and heal the energy of the planet.

Quantum Purpose: To hold the energy template of what's to come and to clear the vibration of the collective consciousness.

Strategy: Wait for recognition and invitation for the big things in life:

- Friendships and Romance
- Career/Work Opportunities
- Where to Live

Emotional Theme: Bitterness is a vital signal for the Orchestrator. When an Orchestrator feels bitter it means that they are not feeling valued or appreciated or they are depleted and exhausted. Bitterness is a "repelling" energy. It can push people away which can be a hidden blessing for the Orchestrator. This isn't personal. It's simply an energetic signal that an Orchestrator needs to reconnect and heal their personal sense of worth so that they can set better boundaries. It's also a way for the Orchestrator to create alone time to regenerate and rest so that they're ready for the next opportunity. They need to remember to be patient and trust in the process of divine timing.

Potential Challenge: Self-worth and energy; feeling abandoned by Spirit.

• The Calibrator •

Calibrator (Reflector)
1 Percent of the Population

Calibrators are wise, intuitive, empathic, and sensitive Lunar beings. They are fully open to the world and to others. They sense and feel the potential of humanity.

Because they have no defined centers by design, they take in the energy of everybody else and see the world through others' eyes, sampling a frequency of energy and reflecting it back. This means they magnify and reflect all that is around them and mirror it back to others. It's through the reflection of what they are showing the world that shows us what we need to recalibrate.

It's essential for Calibrators to choose their partners and friends carefully because they will have a huge impact on their feelings and experience of themselves. Like the other open Sacral Types, Initiators (Manifestors) and Orchestrators (Projectors), they are not here to work in the traditional way like the Alchemists (Generators) and Time Benders (Manifesting Generators), who have a defined Sacral.

They may feel alone and misunderstood and also feel deep disappointment with having to wait and live through the energy of others. It is not correct for Calibrators to make decisions with their mind or like the other Types. They need to experience a choice or decision over a cycle of the Moon, which spans twenty-nine days.

They experience this choice or decision inside of themselves through talking it out over the entire Moon cycle and this gives them the power to be able to realize solutions and the right choices.

Spiritual Purpose: To be the barometer of the alignment of humanity with heart.

Quantum Purpose: To mirror to others the human condition and human potential. It's vital for them to geographically be in the right place with the right people.

Strategy: Waiting twenty-nine days, one full Lunar cycle, to make their decisions. They need and will get clarity over time.

Emotional Theme: Disappointment due to witnessing the unfulfilled potential and the need for more time.

Potential Challenge: Lacking courage and faith to extricate from the misaligned. They see the potential in others so strongly that sometimes they will stay in places and relationships longer than is good for them, healthy, or in their best interest.

Authority

Although decision-making is tied directly to your Strategy, your Authority flavors the way you use your Strategy. Your defined centers will determine your Authority. Not all centers carry Authority, so your personal Authority will depend on your Type and your definition.

Authority will also depend on the conditioning in your life and your level of emotional well-being. When you receive a Human Design reading, you are taught to understand patterns of pain and behaviors that may be keeping you from living out the beauty of the mythology of who you really are.

With cognitive awareness of old patterns, you begin to heal and transform these energies into deep sources of wisdom: The more you clear your old energy patterns, the more effectively your natural decision-making skills, your Authority, can function. You can then begin to use your Authority along with your Strategy to help you make better decisions for your life.

It's very important to note that Authority does *not* override your Strategy, it just shifts the way you use your Strategy so that your decisions and choices are even more in alignment with the overall energy in your Design. Authority influences what you need and, in some cases, the timing to use your Strategy effectively to help you make decisions. Depending on which software you use to generate your Human Design chart, there are many different ways to talk about Authority.

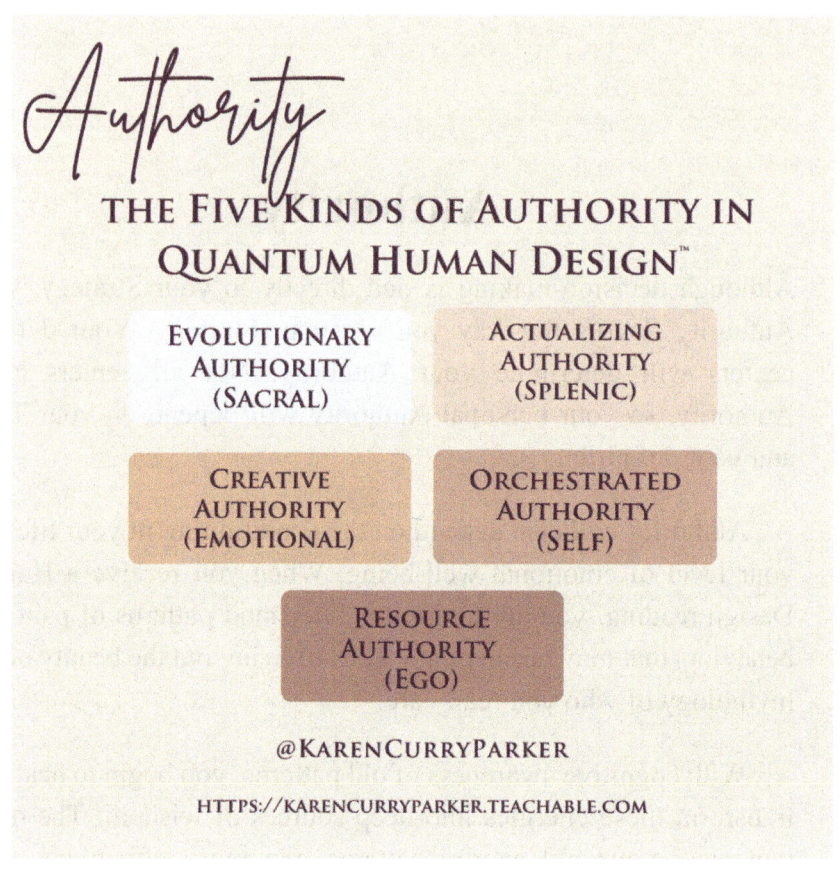

Authority

THE FIVE KINDS OF AUTHORITY IN QUANTUM HUMAN DESIGN™

EVOLUTIONARY
AUTHORITY
(SACRAL)

ACTUALIZING
AUTHORITY
(SPLENIC)

CREATIVE
AUTHORITY
(EMOTIONAL)

ORCHESTRATED
AUTHORITY
(SELF)

RESOURCE
AUTHORITY
(EGO)

@KARENCURRYPARKER

HTTPS://KARENCURRYPARKER.TEACHABLE.COM

All Generator Types (if they have an open Emotional Solar Plexus) have Sacral Authority, called **Evolutionary Authority** in Quantum Human Design™. When you have Sacral Authority, it means that your gut-level response in the moment is letting you know whether something is right for you or not. The biggest challenge with Evolutionary Authority is learning to trust your instinctual response. To learn more about Evolutionary Authority please read the Alchemist and Time Bender Sections.

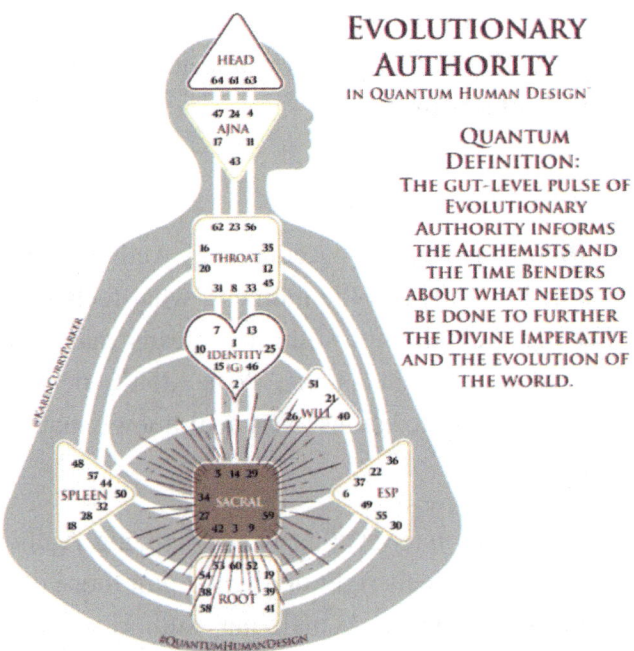

EVOLUTIONARY AUTHORITY
IN QUANTUM HUMAN DESIGN

QUANTUM DEFINITION: THE GUT-LEVEL PULSE OF EVOLUTIONARY AUTHORITY INFORMS THE ALCHEMISTS AND THE TIME BENDERS ABOUT WHAT NEEDS TO BE DONE TO FURTHER THE DIVINE IMPERATIVE AND THE EVOLUTION OF THE WORLD.

Quantum Definition: The gut-level pulse of Evolutionary Authority informs the Alchemists and the Time Benders about what needs to be done to further the divine imperative and the evolution of the world. Initiators (Manifestors), Orchestrators (Projectors), Alchemists (Generators), and Time Benders (Manifesting Generators) all have Authority in their Design. Calibrators (Reflectors), because they have no centers defined in their Design, have no true Authority other than their Calibrator Strategy, which is to wait a full Lunar cycle.

For the sake of of keeping it simple, there are four other basic kinds of Authority:

1. Actualizing Authority (Splenic Authority)
2. Creative Authority (Emotional Authority)
3. Orchestrated Authority (Self Authority)
4. Resource Authority (Ego Authority)

Different Human Design software programs will list other kinds of Authority, but these variations are simply sub-categories of the **five basic kinds of Authority.**

1. Actualizing Authority—Actualizing Authority means that you are designed to know, in the moment, what feels right to you (or not). Having Actualizing Authority means that you can be spontaneous with your decisions. You don't need time to contemplate or sit with decisions. You will know what is true for you immediately.

Much like Evolutionary Authority, Actualizing Authority is a gut-level sense of what feels right or aligned. For those of you who are not Evolutionary Types, Actualizing Authority can help you make smaller decisions about your daily life choices.

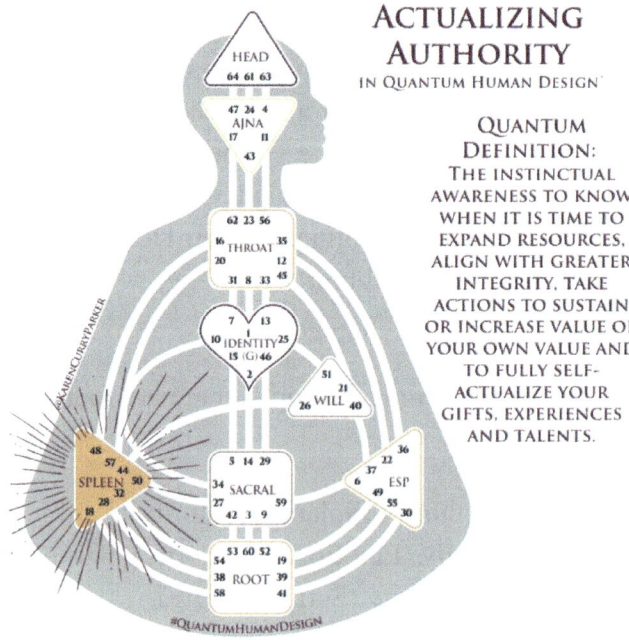

ACTUALIZING AUTHORITY
IN QUANTUM HUMAN DESIGN

QUANTUM DEFINITION: THE INSTINCTUAL AWARENESS TO KNOW WHEN IT IS TIME TO EXPAND RESOURCES, ALIGN WITH GREATER INTEGRITY, TAKE ACTIONS TO SUSTAIN OR INCREASE VALUE OR YOUR OWN VALUE AND TO FULLY SELF-ACTUALIZE YOUR GIFTS, EXPERIENCES AND TALENTS.

For example, if you have Actualizing Authority and you are at the health food store searching for a vitamin supplement, your Self-Actualization Center might give you a sense of which vitamin is right for you.

Often we recognize Actualizing Authority in hindsight. Actualizing Authority is that feeling of "knowing" something is right or wrong and, upon reflection, realizing you should have listened to yourself. With practice, you can begin to notice your Actualizing Authority in the moment, allowing the wisdom and awareness of your intuition to guide you and give you essential insights about what you need.

Quantum Definition: The instinctual awareness to know when it is time to expand resources, align with greater integrity, take actions to sustain or increase value or your own value, and to fully self-actualize your gifts, experiences, and talents.

2. Creative Authority—If you have Creative Authority, you are not designed to be spontaneous. You need time to make decisions, and learning how to wait for clarity is essential to help you not experience disappointment in your life's choices.

Creative Authority can influence the way the Strategy for your Type works. Your Strategy for your Type is still essential, but if you have Creative Authority, it means you have to check in with your Strategy and sense how you feel over time.

When you have Creative Authority, you tend to have a lot of emotional energy. You are passionate and experience big feelings to various degrees depending on other aspects of your chart. (For more insights, read the section on the Creativity Center.)

This internal emotional energy makes it essential that you take your time to make decisions. It's easy to leap into things in the moment when they feel good only to wake up the next day doubting whether you made the right choice. Waiting for clarity helps avoid some of the regrets you may have experienced in your life.

With Creative Authority, your decision has to stay consistent over time. If you are all over the place with how you feel about your choice during the course of waiting for clarity, it's probably not the right decision to make.

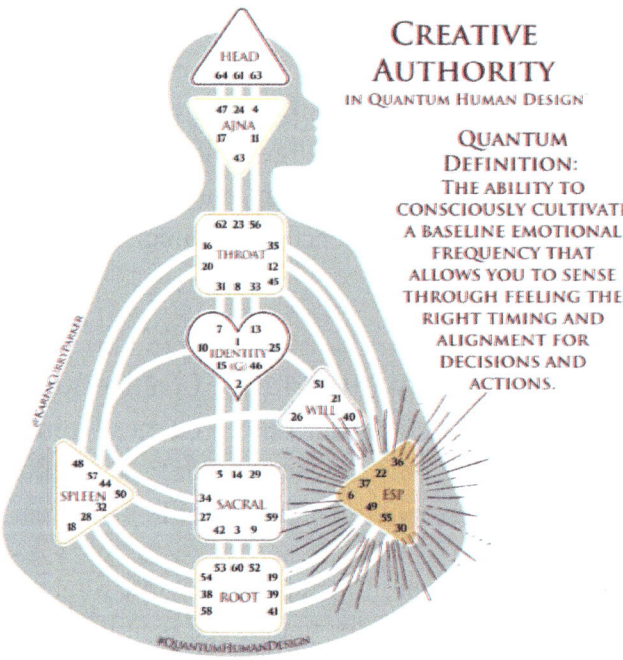

Here's how this might look. Let's say you get invited to speak at an event sponsored by a group that you like but you're not crazy about. You love speaking but you don't necessarily enjoy this particular group. When you get the invitation, you're so excited to land a speaking gig, that you immediately accept the invitation. The next morning when you wake up, you question your decision, and you have a small anxiety stomachache from worrying about whether you did the right thing.

Over the next couple of days, you try to talk yourself into believing that it was the right choice. You manage to stir up enthusiasm along the way, but you can't quite get your energy aligned with the opportunity. When you finally give the talk, several group members want to hire you, but they end up being clients you don't really enjoy, and you're left continuing to feel obligated to do business in a way that doesn't feel good to you.

If you had followed your Creative Authority, when you got invited to speak, you might have answered, "Thank you. This sounds like a lovely invitation. I need to check my calendar and get back to you. When do you need to know my response?"

Your answer would have bought you time to really check in with your feelings to see if this was the right choice for you, and you would have been aligned with whatever felt correct.

The most important thing to remember with Creative Authority is that your decision has to stay consistent over time. If you feel a yes in response to an opportunity, that yes has to stay true over the course of a couple of days. If you're all over the place with your feelings, it's not the right decision for you.

Quantum Definition: The ability to consciously cultivate a baseline emotional frequency that allows you to sense through feeling the right timing and alignment for decisions and actions.

3. Orchestrated Authority—This Authority is kind of a catch-all phrase for a few different, less common Authorities. If you have a chart that says Self-Projected Authority, No Authority, No Inner

Authority, or Mental-Projected Authority, it simply means that you need to talk through your choices to get clarity.

ORCHESTRATED AUTHORITY
IN QUANTUM HUMAN DESIGN

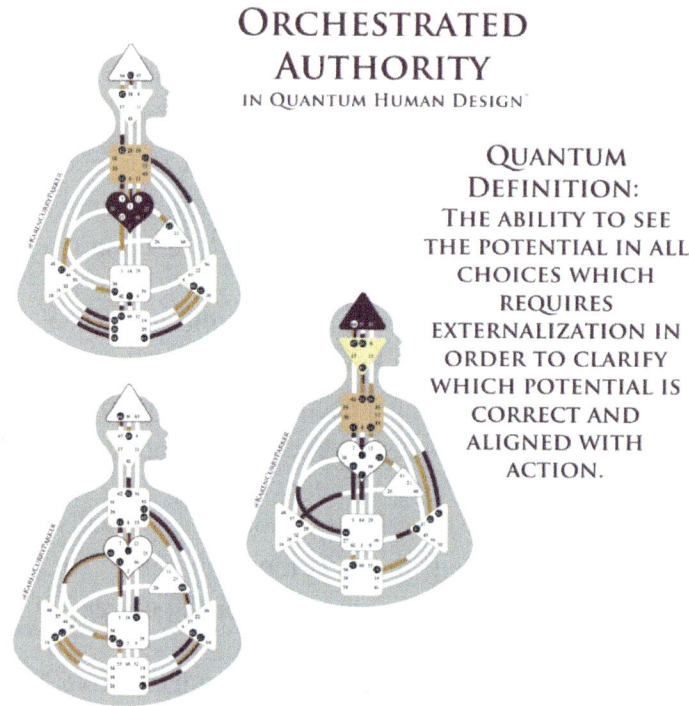

QUANTUM DEFINITION:
THE ABILITY TO SEE THE POTENTIAL IN ALL CHOICES WHICH REQUIRES EXTERNALIZATION IN ORDER TO CLARIFY WHICH POTENTIAL IS CORRECT AND ALIGNED WITH ACTION.

You don't need advice. You simply need a sounding board, a good friend or someone you trust who can listen to you while you talk through your options. When you have this kind of Authority, it means that you are gifted in seeing the potential of all possibilities. Talking it out helps you decide which potential possibilities are the ones you want to follow.

Orchestrated Authority is common for Orchestrator Types and for all Calibrators.

Quantum Definition: The ability to see the potential in all choices and the need to talk it out in order to clarify which potential is correct and aligned with action.

4. Resource Authority—Having this Authority means that you have a defined Resource Center, and you don't have Creative Authority.

Because the Resource Center is about having sustainable energy and resources (or not!), if you have Resource Authority, it means that you won't decide to do something unless you have the energy or the resources. It also can signal whether a choice is aligned with integrity or not.

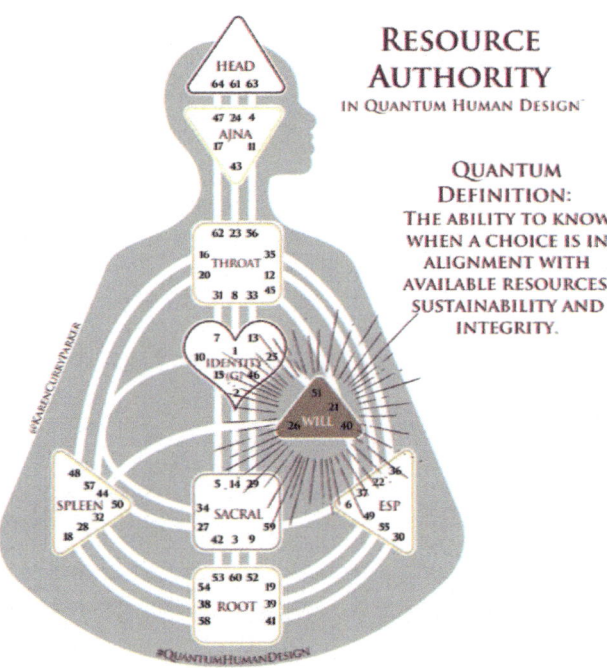

RESOURCE AUTHORITY
IN QUANTUM HUMAN DESIGN

QUANTUM DEFINITION: THE ABILITY TO KNOW WHEN A CHOICE IS IN ALIGNMENT WITH AVAILABLE RESOURCES, SUSTAINABILITY AND INTEGRITY.

This can present a challenge sometimes because it means that you have to have healthy self-worth in order to be comfortable saying no to something if you don't have the energy or the resources for it or if something about the decisions feels out of integrity. If you're in a pattern of trying to prove your worth by pleasing others, you may find that you have to strengthen your sense of value before you can truly follow the Authority of your Resource Center.

Quantum Definition: The ability to know when a choice is in alignment with available resources, sustainability, and integrity.

The Nine Centers

The first thing you may notice when you look at your chart is that there are nine geometric shapes. These are called the nine centers.

Each center carries and manages a certain frequency of energy and relates to specific themes in our lives.

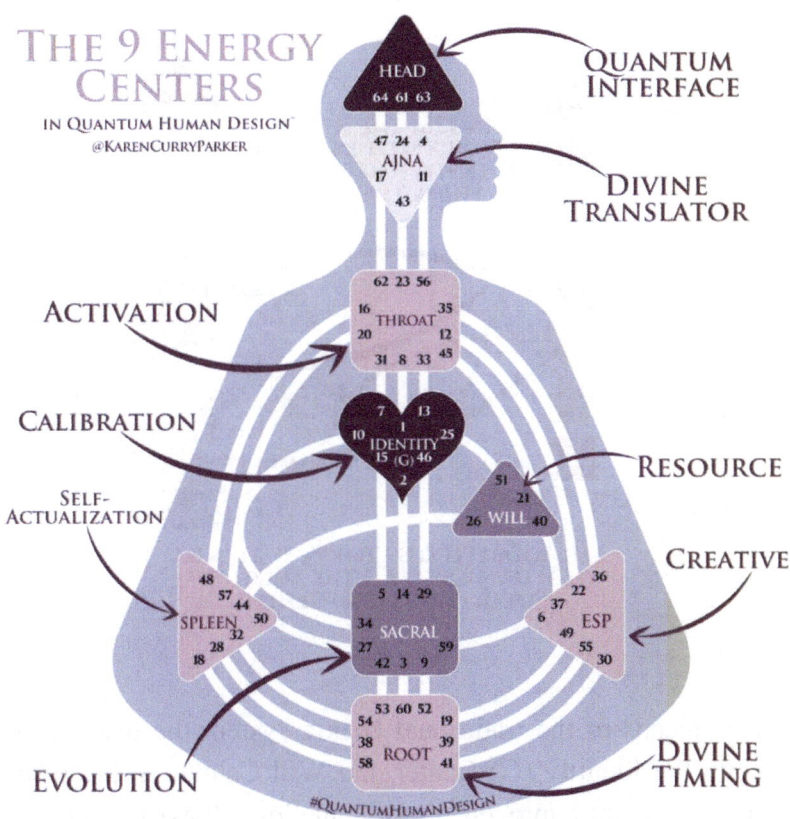

The Transition from Seven-Centered to Nine-Centered Beings

With the discovery of the planet Uranus by Herschel in 1781, we moved into the Uranian era when human beings with highly evolved nine-centered forms began replacing the seven-centered, mind-oriented beings. By the late 1800s, the process was complete, making all of us alive today as nine-centered beings.

TRANSITION FROM 7-CENTERED TO 9-CENTERED BEINGS

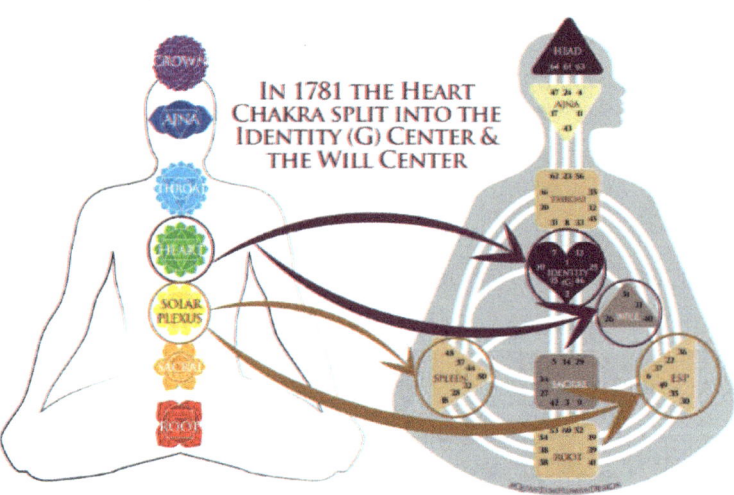

In 1781 the Heart Chakra split into the Identity (G) Center & the Will Center

The Solar Plexus Chakra split into the Spleen Center & the Emotional Solar Plexus (ESP) Center

@KARENCURRYPARKER

This means in the traditional chakra system the heart chakra split into the Identity (G) Center and Will Center. And the solar plexus chakra split into the Emotional Solar Plexus Center and Spleen Center.

This historically significant moment in our evolution marked the movement away from our need to focus on survival through the mental awareness, or mental intelligence, of the strategic mind.

The seven-centered beings had a shorter life expectancy marked by the Saturnian cycle. Our new nine-centered forms or bodies have an eighty-four-year life expectancy marked by the Uranian cycle.

Seven-centered beings were driven to find connection and communion through sexuality because of the need and desire to reproduce whereas now, as nine-centered beings, we are finding connection and communion through awareness.

Our highly evolved nine-centered body vehicle is designed to guide us through life decision by decision, meaning we no longer need to look to an outer authority through our mind for direction. There are no answers in our minds, only infinite possibilities.

Understanding our Human Design Type, Strategy, and Authority allows us to make decisions that are correctly in alignment with our most authentic self, which then, as we practice this, allows us to trust ourselves more and more.

• Defined Centers •

If a center is colored, then it is called *defined*. A defined center has a consistent way of operating and is part of the energy you consistently express. This is the energy that you radiate out into the world.

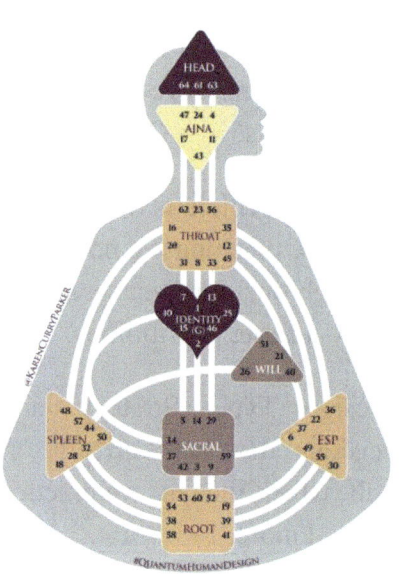

It operates the same way energetically and thematically. This is the aspect of your personality that is true all the time, independent of any other factors in your environment.

Your definition is determined by what gates the planets were transiting in at the moment of your birth. Your definition will stay the same throughout your lifetime.

The beauty of our defined and open centers is that individually we are all puzzle pieces—parts of a greater whole. We all become completely defined when we are all together.

We each bring pieces that energetically unify us all and offer us the opportunity to express all of the human experience.

We all have *all* of the chart. What is defined in your chart is what you consistently experience, radiate, and express all the time no matter where you are, who you're with , or where the planets are transiting.

The way that you are defined and your specific configuration (energetic hardwiring) is completely unique to you and you alone, there is no one else exactly like you on the planet—similar... sure, but not exactly like you.

You're a once-in-a-lifetime cosmic event and that makes you rare, precious, special, and an *invaluable vital gift* to the entire planet!

• Open Centers •

If a center is white, then it is called *open*—previouly referred to as *undefined*.

Open Center = A white center with at least one gate activation (called a hanging gate).

Completely Open Center = A white center with no gate activation (no hanging gates).

Open centers are where we take in energy and information from the world around us. We not only absorb various energies in our openness, but we also *amplify* them.

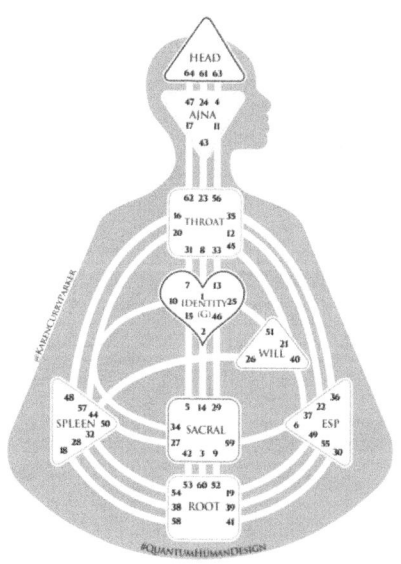

In our openness, we experience other people's energies and because of this, we have the potential for great wisdom but also the potential for pain and confusion. It's in our openness that we have been deeply conditioned by family, friends, and society.

These open areas represent aspects of your personality that are inconsistent because it changes depending on who you're around. This can also feel more intense than defined energy because it's always changing and you're amplifying it.

It's easy to think the energy in your open centers is yours, and sometimes you will try to "fix" an aspect of your personality or wonder *What's wrong with me?* not realizing that you're behaving according to outside factors that aren't even really you!

Your openness is where you have the potential for the most pain until you understand how your energy works; until you learn what *is* you/yours and what's *not* you/yours.

When you learn what energy is yours and what isn't yours is when your openness starts to become the place for your greatest wisdom. You learn that you're only experiencing this energy and it's not what defines you. You're then able to experience the energy and let it go.

Are you aware of the areas you've been conditioned? Having this awareness starts the deconditioning process.

• The Quantum Interface (Head) Center •

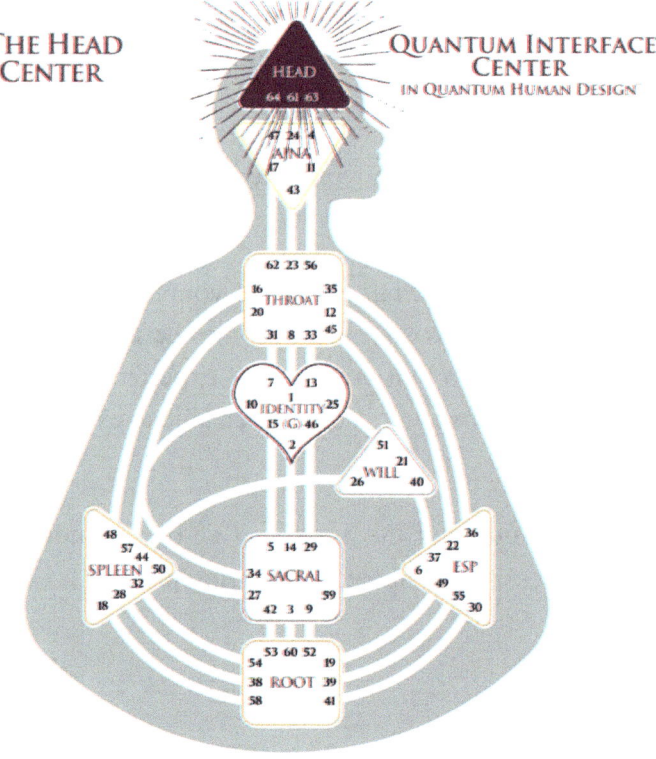

THE HEAD
CENTER

QUANTUM INTERFACE
CENTER
IN QUANTUM HUMAN DESIGN

Because the energy in the defined Head Center is always on, people with defined Head Centers are inspirational forces on the planet. They're always radiating inspiration out into the world and may not even be aware of it because it's happening energetically, but it's happening.

Defined Head Centers have a consistent source of inspiration. They are always asking questions and may feel like something's wrong, experience confusion, or struggle to know what to do if they don't have the answers.

Inspiration is a reflective process, it's important to process the questions you are receiving, but *don't* rely on the answers to make decisions about your life, follow your Strategy instead!

Oftentimes people with defined Head Centers don't realize that they're even questioning things. They may even have a permanent quizzical look on their face; it's simply a part of their consistent energy.

Affirmation for your defined Head Center: "I am inspired and inspiring. I spread inspiration everywhere I go, and I share my ideas and inspirations with others according to my Strategy."

Someone with an open Head Center does not have a consistent way of receiving inspiration, so when they come across inspiration, they will take it in and amplify it. It's very easy when you have an open Head Center to feel inspired all the time. Not only do you feel inspired, but you also feel pressure to act on this inspiration.

Those who understand their open Head Center can have a very deep understanding of who and what is truly inspiring. They can be wise about which inspirations to take action on and which to simply observe.

Not only will someone with an open Head Center have the ability to take in the inspiration of the world and amplify it, but they'll also take in all the questions of the world and amplify those too.

Remember, you do not need to answer any of the questions. The only thing you really need to do to make good decisions is to follow your Strategy!

The purpose is not to try and figure things out, it's to use the power of your daydreams and imagination—your creative thinking—to stimulate emotional energy. That emotional energy in turn calibrates your Heart Center and the electromagnetic resonance field of the heart creates a vibrational frequency that attracts into your life things that match that particular frequency of creativity.

Calibrating emotional energy and using the power of your thoughts maintains and sustains a high-quality emotional frequency of energy to support you in creating what you want in your life.

Question to ask yourself with an open Head Center: "Am I under pressure to answer other people's questions and live out their ideas and inspirations?"

Affirmation for your open Head Center: "I am deeply inspired all the time. I am wise about what is truly inspiring. I follow my Strategy to help me decide what I need to do. The questions in my head are from others. I don't have to answer all of them, only the ones that truly excite me!"

• The Divine Translator (Ajna) Center •

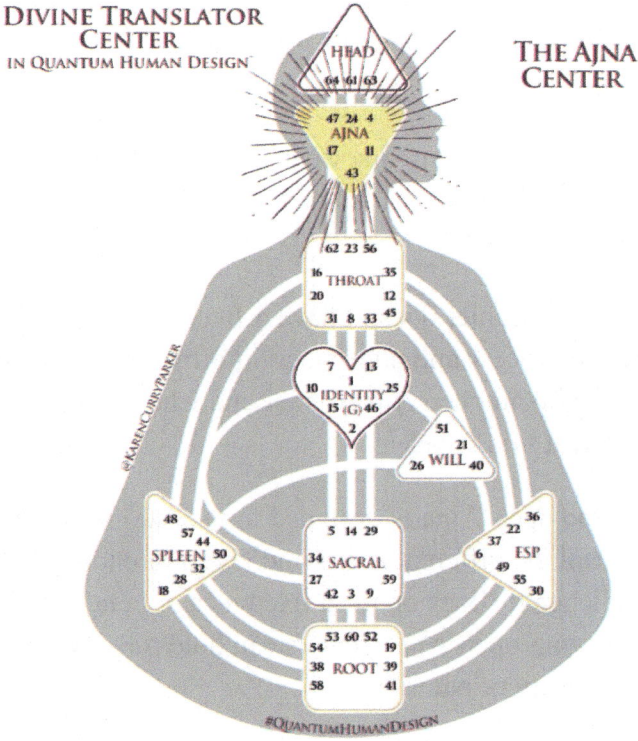

The defined Ajna Center is designed to hold information. It is trustworthy and reliable, but it is fixed in how it works. It's important to remember that the mind is a great resource, but it is *not* a place to make decisions; no decisions should come from the mind. That's what your Strategy and Authority is for.

If your Ajna is defined, try playing and experimenting in your relationships to only share or speak what's on your mind if you're asked to share or if someone asks you what you think, especially if it's giving your opinion. This works both ways, you can also ask "Hey, would you like to hear what I think?" Or "Can I share something that's on my mind with you?" You may find that what you have to say is more well-received.

Affirmation for your defined Ajna Center: "I am gentle with my thinking and always remember that there are many ways to think about information. I am uniquely capable of being certain. I listen carefully to the thoughts of others and allow for limitless thinking with grace."

Someone with an open Ajna Center can see many sides to an issue. They are fair, judicious, empathetic, open-minded, and can also be very intellectual.

An open Ajna Center doesn't have a fixed way of thinking, so they are able to process and understand information in a myriad of ways. People with an open Ajna Center and who are able to relax, can become great mind readers.

Because the open Ajna is designed to take in information and ideas and see all the different layers and levels of understanding, it can be a challenge to "lock on to" a fixed idea or belief. With great effort, people with open Ajna Centers can hold a fixed idea, but it doesn't come easily or naturally.

You may have been told that you need to just make up your mind about something and stick to it. Remember that you are here to be wise about ideas and beliefs, but not necessarily adopt them. The beliefs that you hold on to will be the ones you came to through using your Human Design Strategy and Authority.

Question to ask yourself with an open Ajna Center: "Am I struggling with making up my mind or feeling confident in my decisions? Am I trying to convince others and myself that I am certain?"

Affirmation for your open Ajna Center: "I am wise about information and beliefs. My gift is that I can see many sides of an issue and have many different understandings that are fluid and that change all the time. I don't have to make up my mind. I always write down the things I want to remember."

• The Activation (Throat) Center •

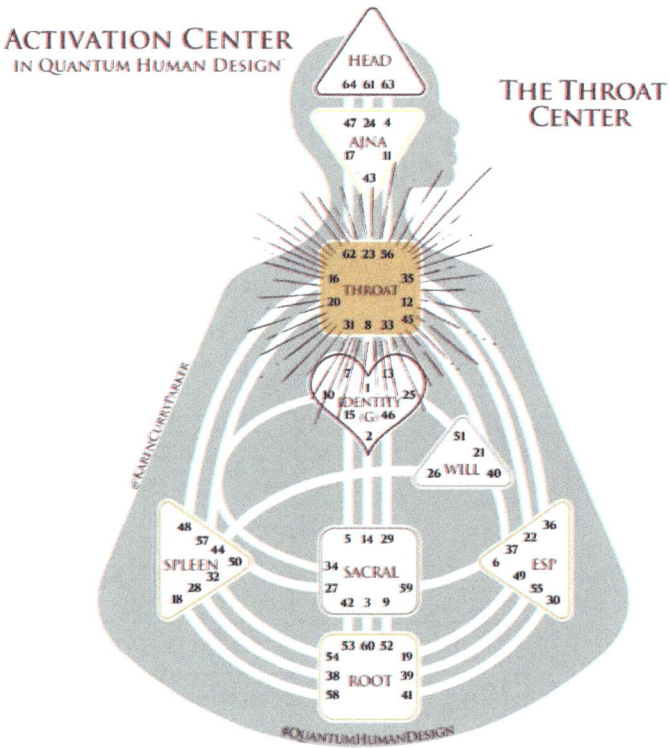

The defined Throat Center is designed to speak, but how it speaks is controlled by what it is connected to. Effective communication is vital for personal and global well-being. Experiment with living your Strategy and see how it improves the quality of your relationships.

Throat Connections

It's vital to enter into communication correctly.

- Initiators (Manifestors) and Time Benders (Manifesting Generators) can initiate speaking.

- Alchemists (Generators) need to wait to respond to speak. You work and relate (you speak and act on the responsive sounds of the Sacral about work and relationships).
- Orchestrators (Projectors) need to wait to be invited to speak.
- Calibrators (Reflectors) also need to be asked (or invited/called out/recognized) to speak as well.

Throat Connection Themes

Ajna to the Throat: You speak your mind but should only do so when you are asked and invited.

Spleen to the Throat: You talk about what you sense, you are highly intuitive, and you want to go deep.

G Center to the Throat: You are what you talk about, speaking from the depth of who you are, your soul. You can be very vulnerable and sensitive to criticism, as your creative expression comes straight from your identity. If you're judged for who you are, you can go into a shell like a turtle and shut down.

Will to the Throat: You talk about yourself, "I this, I that" (me, me, me). You have the potential to be in ego or surrender who you are to serve others in deep service and providing resources for others, but will always talk using the pronoun *I*.

Emotional Solar Plexus to the Throat: You talk about what you feel and can speak about your emotions easily.

Root to the Throat: You talk about what you do (the drive to do/timing and sense). *Tip:* Projected energy (non-motorized energy) needs to be invited or asked to speak in order to be heard.

Sacral to the Throat: Your natural impulse is to "do" often before you find the words to explain what it is you're doing to others. This configuration works best when you respond to an experience or event and then make sure you tell the people around you what you're going to do before you go do it.

Affirmation for your Defined Throat: "I speak with great responsibility and know the true source of my words. I allow others to have a voice, and I use my words to invite others to share."

People with an open Throat Center always feel under pressure to speak. When they are in a group or in school this can be very difficult. The open Throat often blurts out comments or answers—sometimes uncontrollably—unaware of where the comment came from (this can be even worse if your Ajna is also open).

There is, however, deep wisdom in the open Throat Center. Many great singers (like Celine Dion) and well-known speakers (like Oprah Winfrey) have open Throat Centers. Someone with an open Throat can speak in various ways depending on who they are with. They can be very good at speaking foreign languages and impersonating others' speech.

In order for the open Throat and the thyroid to remain healthy, it is important to speak according to your Strategy. Try experimenting with not talking; don't say a thing unless you're given something to respond to or you are invited into a conversation. If you are silent, your aura does the talking! Just wait and see. People won't be able to stop themselves from talking to you!

Question to ask yourself with an open Throat Center: "Am I trying to get attention so that I can be heard?"

Affirmation for your open Throat Center: "My words are heard best when I am invited to speak. I save my words for people who truly desire to hear my point of view and insights. I wait for the right people to ask me and value my words."

• The Calibration (Identity/G) Center •

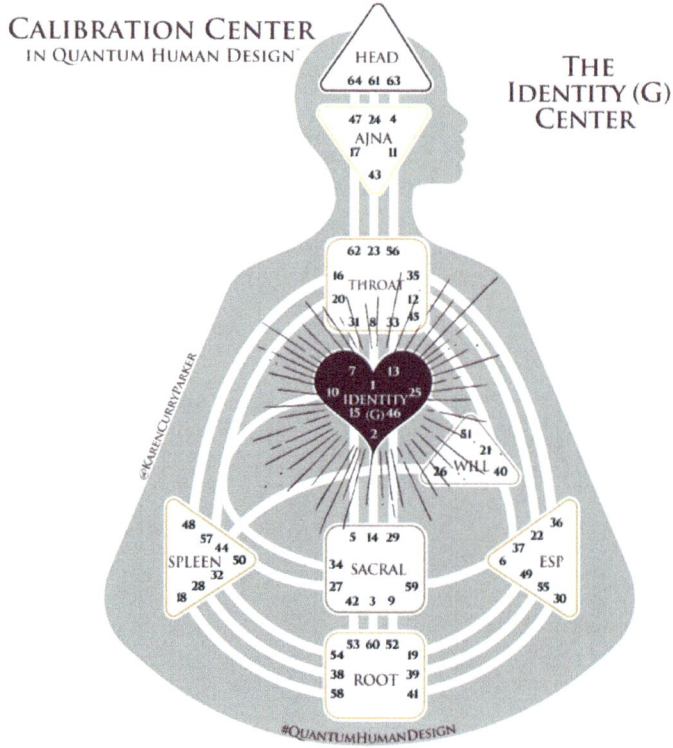

CALIBRATION CENTER
IN QUANTUM HUMAN DESIGN

THE IDENTITY (G) CENTER

HEAD
64 61 63

47 24 4
AJNA
17 11
43

62 23 56
16 35
THROAT
20 12
31 8 33 45

7 13
10 25
IDENTITY
15 (G) 46
2
51
21
26 WILL 40

48
57 44
SPLEEN 50
32
28
18

5 14 29
34 SACRAL
27 59
42 3 9

36
22
37
6 ESP
49 55
30

53 60 52
54 19
38 ROOT 39
58 41

@KARENCURRYPARKER

#QUANTUMHUMANDESIGN

In 1781 the heart chakra split in two, the Identity (G) Center and Will Center.

We calibrate our heart by virtue of the quality of love that we are experiencing for ourselves and in our lives. Not just love, but love and acceptance. Self-love and self-acceptance really are the big energies associated with the G Center.

Self-acceptance is the theme of the soul curriculum when our G Center is defined. Both self-love and self-acceptance are calibrated by the gates of the G Center.

We are designed to take our direction in life or what we attract into our life based on the magnetic resonance field of our heart which is an attractive force otherwise known as the Magnetic Monopole.

We attract into our life things that match the quality of love that we have. The highest expression of all the archetypes amplifies the potential direction that our life takes us.

The more we know and understand these energies and live out the optimal expressions, the richer our life gets and the richer the things we attract become.

Love, in one form or another, is what life is all about. The feeling of separation is what drives us to look outside ourselves for love, trying to get a sense of where we are going and who we are in relation to others. We are trying to become worthy of the illusive love we seek.

The truth is that everything has been right here within us all along; we do not have to look outside ourselves to discover who we are, or where to go to find love. The G Center holds love. Love is the force that permeates and binds the Universe, pulling everything toward a state of oneness again.

Surrendering to the direction of our form is how we are designed to experience the fullness of that love. We are not here to be loved, but to *be love*.

Affirmation for your defined Identity (G) Center: "I am who I am. I express myself in all that I do. I celebrate the magnificence of who I am."

The aspects or archetypes that influence the kind of love we are experiencing (or not) in our lives include the following:

Gate 10: Self-Love—Empowering others to love themselves by example.

Gate 7: Collaboration—Natural ability to support a leader in fulfilling their role to better serve the people they're leading. (Chief of Staff type energy.)

Gate 1: Purpose—Wisdom to realize that the full expression of your unique potential *is* the creative gift you give to the world.

Gate 13: Narrative—Capacity to craft a powerful personal narrative and for doing forgiveness work. Hearing and holding stories of others, finding the gifts in the stories, and taking those blessings from the past to use as a source of growth and expansion. To reframe the story so that it serves the highest good and well-being of all.

Gate 25: Spirit (Trusting the Universe)—Direction in life that is influenced by trusting the Universe and knowing you are loved by Spirit and the Universe. Ability to find spiritual blessing and connection in every aspect of life. Healing by remembering your connection to Spirit and surrendering the ego (self) to your higher-self (soul).

Gate 46: Embodiment—Recognition that your body is the vehicle for your soul. Loving your body and holding your physical form as a sacred vessel for the essence of your soul and embodying within your vessel the sacredness of who you are. To fully experience and express the full vitality of Spirit in form.

Gate 2: Allowing—Ability to allow and receive greater and greater things because you are worth it and deserve it. To value, love, and accept yourself and align with being fully supported by the Universe in all the ways you need in order to fulfill your life purpose.

Gate 15: Compassion—A place of compassion and love for self and others. Following the flow of natural order and finding the place to serve the greatest needs.

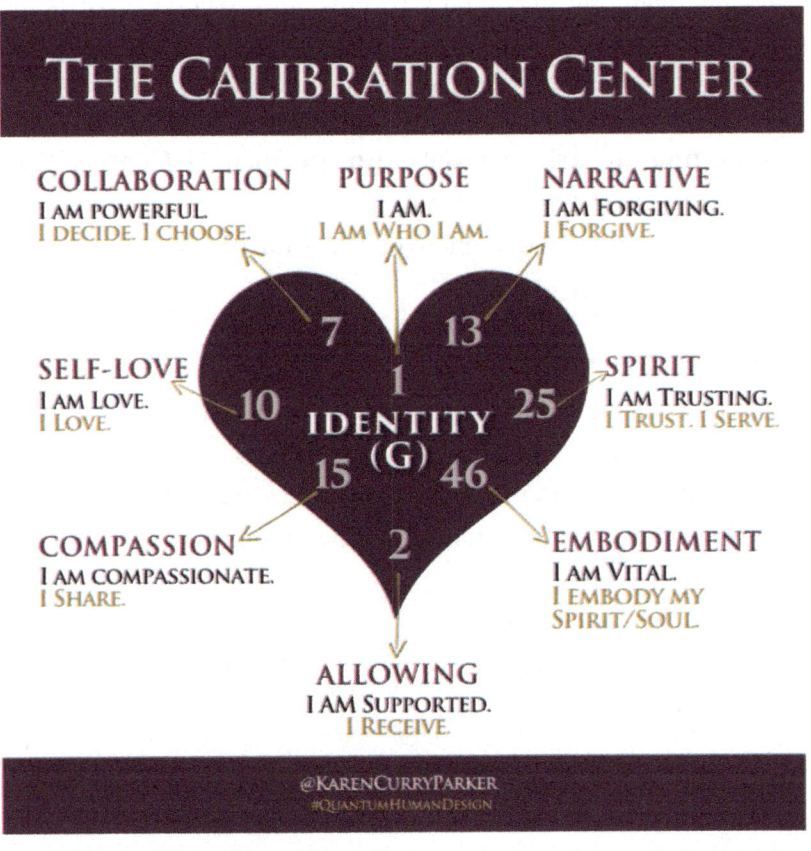

THE CALIBRATION CENTER

COLLABORATION
I AM POWERFUL.
I DECIDE. I CHOOSE.

PURPOSE
I AM.
I AM WHO I AM.

NARRATIVE
I AM FORGIVING.
I FORGIVE.

7   13

SELF-LOVE
I AM LOVE.
I LOVE.

10   1   25

SPIRIT
I AM TRUSTING.
I TRUST. I SERVE.

IDENTITY
(G)
15   46

COMPASSION
I AM COMPASSIONATE.
I SHARE.

2

EMBODIMENT
I AM VITAL.
I EMBODY MY
SPIRIT/SOUL

ALLOWING
I AM SUPPORTED.
I RECEIVE.

@KARENCURRYPARKER
#QUANTUMHUMANDESIGN

People with an open G Center understand other people's sense of self and direction. They'll take in another person's identity and amplify it, giving them insight into another person's perspective.

It is extremely important for people with open G Centers to geographically be in the right place and with the right people. How they express themselves may change depending on who they are experiencing at the moment.

Because a person with an open G Center has a dynamic sense of themselves and their own personal direction, often they can be afraid that they're not lovable. Who they perceive themselves to be is always changing and therefore how they receive love is also always changing. Children with an open G Center may also sometimes be a little bit more vulnerable to self-esteem issues.

Questions to ask yourself with an open G Center: "Do I question my lovability? Am I struggling to find direction? Do I love where I live, where I work, and who I'm with? Am I taking on other people's personalities?"

Affirmation for your open G Center: "How I experience myself changes depending on who I am with. I choose to surround myself with people who feel good to me. Place is very important to me, and I create an environment that soothes me. When I am in the right place, the right opportunities come to me."

• The Resource (Will) Center •

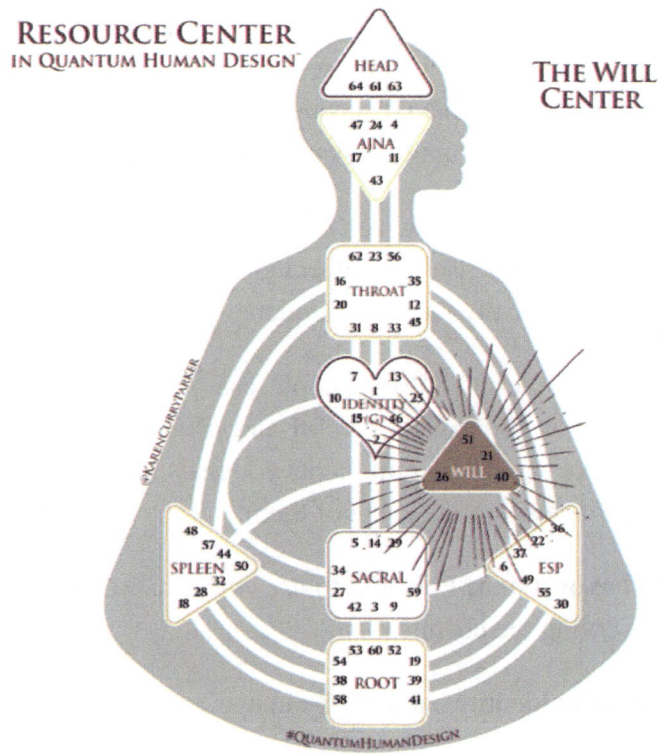

RESOURCE CENTER
IN QUANTUM HUMAN DESIGN

THE WILL
CENTER

When you have a defined Will Center, you have consistent access to willpower. You can be willful. This aspect of our identity is an individuated part of our unique expression that is in service to the greater good.

The defined Will Center is designed to work and then rest. Generally speaking, if you have an open Sacral, but your Will is defined, it is very important to take time off or go on vacation periodically; if you push too hard without rest, you may end up with heart troubles or stomach problems. *(Of course, it also depends on what else you have going on in your Design.)*

If you have a defined Will Center, you will energetically empower others by making them feel as if they can do anything. And they can, as long as they are standing in your aura.

Be gentle with others who don't seem to be able to do things the way you can. The truth is that most people don't have willpower and need to enter into their commitments in a different way than you.

In the defined Will Center, you have the ability to surrender to personal self (ego) and rise up connected to Source (higher self), i.e., my will = ego vs. thy will = surrender.

Also having a defined Will, people can project promises or commitments onto you. So be careful and clear about what you promise to people and the commitments you make. People will also feel like you will want to take care of them.

Optimal expression: Potential to use who you are in the world as a way of serving the cosmic plan.

Shadow side: Identity can only be in ego.

Allow the natural flow of this energy to carry you rather than try and drag it with your own strength.

Affirmation for your defined Will Center: "It's important for me to rest. Rest allows me to recharge my willpower. I honor the promises that I make. I make deliberate promises and understand that people expect me to keep my promises. I am gentle with my expectations of others. Not everyone can just do the things that I do."

When you have an open Will Center, it's crucial that you use your Strategy to make agreements and promises. If you don't, you'll be using energy you don't have and run the risk of entering into the wrong situations and feeling obligated to make yourself follow through. And you might miss the right opportunity because you'll be busy forcing yourself to do something you really don't want to do.

Because the Will Center is also all about value and the material plane, it's also very common that you may have a tendency to undervalue yourself. It's common for people with open Will Centers to undercharge for their business services or even give their services away for free.

Remember that the open centers are our deepest sources of wisdom. The open Will Center can help you become very wise about what is truly valuable in life. You may, with time and experience, become very wise about what you are worth, both in the area of business and in your personal life. You may also become wise about knowing when it's time to work and when it's time to rest.

You might be wondering, if I don't have willpower, how will I get things done? You can and do get things done, but you have to enter into each of your commitments according to the Strategy for your Type.

When you have an open Will Center, it's very important for you to understand that following your Strategy may save your life. We're all conditioned to believe that we have willpower. We are the "just do it" society. And, of course, if we force ourselves to do it outside our Strategies, we fail and end up feeling lousy and burned out.

Questions to ask yourself with an open Will Center: "Do I feel like I have something to prove? Am I questioning my worth? Am I under-valuing myself?"

Affirmation for your open Will Center: "I enter into all agreements according to my Human Design Strategy. I make promises and commitments very carefully and deliberately, and only according to my Strategy. I have nothing to prove, and I value myself deeply. I fearlessly ask to be paid what I am worth."

• The Creative (Emotional Solar Plexus) Center •

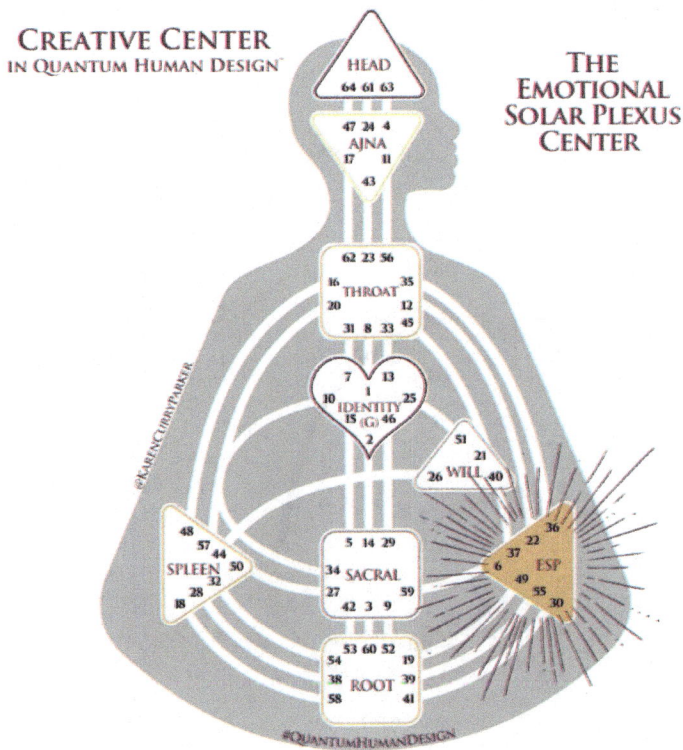

If you're part of the 50 percent of the population that has the Emotional Solar Plexus (ESP) defined, you carry emotional energy at all times.

The channels connecting your Emotional Solar Plexus to other centers will determine the kind of emotional wave(s) that you experience. Some of you may experience high emotional highs and low emotional lows, with plateaus in between. Others will have only small undulations in your emotional frequency, and some may experience a slow ride up and deep plummet down and then it repeats.

Because of the wavelike nature of emotional energy, it is easy to mistake the melancholy of the low end of the wave for depression. If you are emotionally defined, depression can become a big problem if you are looking for a reason why you are feeling down.

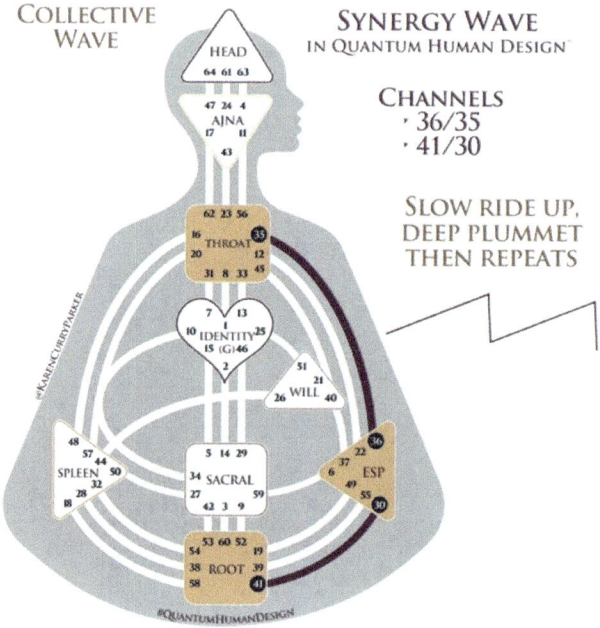

Introduction to Quantum Human Design

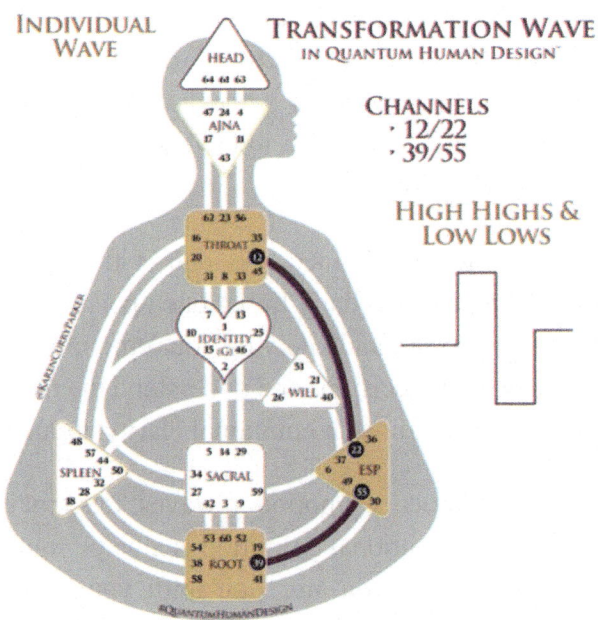

INDIVIDUAL WAVE

TRANSFORMATION WAVE
in Quantum Human Design

CHANNELS
- 12/22
- 39/55

HIGH HIGHS &
LOW LOWS

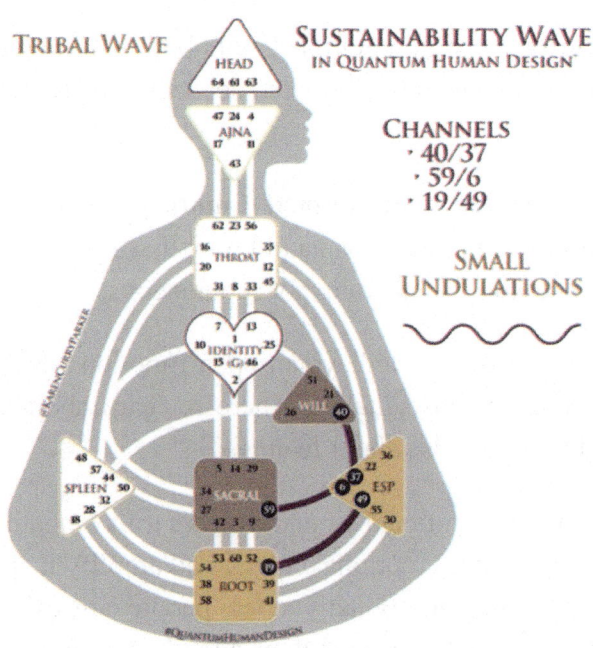

TRIBAL WAVE

SUSTAINABILITY WAVE
in Quantum Human Design

CHANNELS
- 40/37
- 59/6
- 19/49

SMALL
UNDULATIONS

The Nine Centers

We have a lot of judgment against negative emotions in our society. But not all negative emotions are destructive. Melancholy or the low end of an emotional wave is also a very important creative energy. It allows a person to evaluate an issue from many different emotional perspectives.

If you are emotionally defined, it is a good idea to keep a log of your emotional energy on a daily basis. Each person has their own unique emotional rhythm, and knowing your emotional pattern will help you make healthy decisions and understand the timeframe that you may need in order to reach emotional clarity about a decision.

Because you experience emotion in waves, it is crucial that you honor your process. Emotional definition is always your Authority, so no matter what Type you are, wait until you have emotional clarity before you take action or respond. You are not designed to be spontaneous.

Waiting for the right emotional state before taking action will keep you from leaping into emotional decisions and regretting them later.

Affirmation for your defined Emotional Solar Plexus: "I take my time making decisions and know that I reach clarity over time. I am here to be deliberate, not spontaneous."

Fifty percent of people have an open Emotional Solar Plexus. Emotionally open individuals are here to learn about emotional energy and become wise about feelings.

When you are emotionally open, you are truly empathic and can take in other people's emotional energy and amplify it. This can be a great gift. Many emotionally open people are great at sales because they can instantly read their client's emotional status and tailor their sales pitch accordingly.

Because the open Emotional Solar Plexus will take in emotional energy and amplify it, this can be a very painful center to have open when you do not understand how it works. It is easy to think that the emotions you are experiencing are your own, and if someone else's energy is negative, it can be painful when it flows into your awareness.

Consequently, it is common for emotionally open people to develop coping strategies that involve being nice, people-pleasing, avoiding conflict, or having a secret life. It is not that emotionally open people are weak or lack character. It is truly more painful for these people to enter into highly charged emotional situations.

It is crucial to become conscious of emotional energy when you are emotionally open so that you can allow that frequency of energy to flow through you without you feeling responsible for it or as if you need to fix it. Be an emotional screen, not a sponge.

Oftentimes a person who is consistently acting out with great drama is emotionally open. This person is picking up and amplifying the emotional energy of their family and friends. On their own, however, these people are actually quite mild and don't experience a lot of emotional energy.

Question to ask yourself with an open Emotional Solar Plexus: "Am I avoiding truth and conflict and trying to keep everyone happy?"

Affirmation for your Emotional Solar Plexus: "I can make decisions in the moment. I pay attention to the source of my emotions and allow others to experience their feelings without making their experience my own. I'm very sensitive and I trust my insights about other people's feelings. I take frequent breaks when the emotional energy is too intense."

• The Divine Timing (Root) Center •

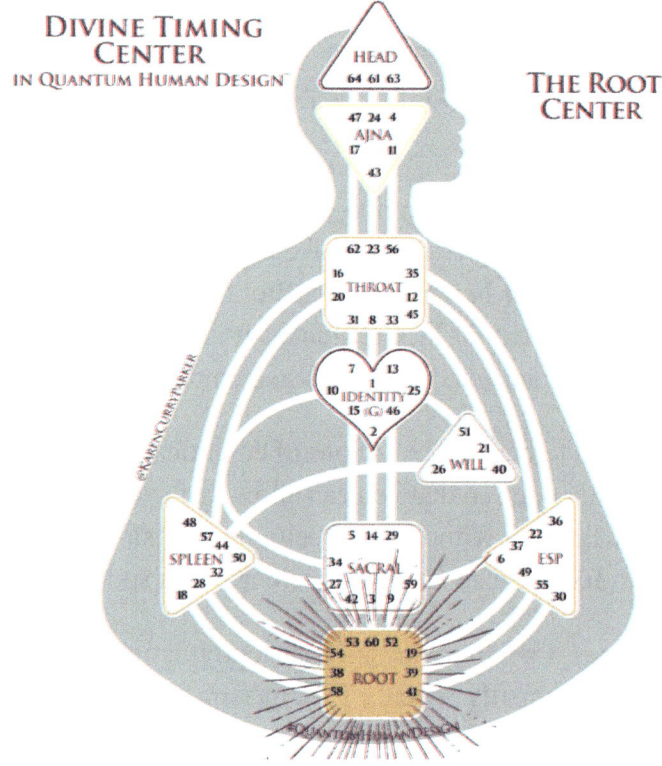

If you have a defined Root Center, this means that you have a fixed way of processing adrenaline energy, and it will operate cyclically, depending on which of the lines you have colored in around your Root Center. You will get things done when the adrenaline pulse is there; when you don't have that adrenaline pulse, things won't necessarily get done.

You have a natural cycle for your adrenaline energy, and you'll have your own unique pulse.

If you have a defined Root Center, you are somewhat immune to adrenaline pressure. That doesn't mean that you don't experience stress.

However, your stress may come from other factors or through other open centers that you may have in your Design. Simply put, when you have a defined Root Center, things get done when they get done.

Root Center Connections

- **Root Center connected to Emotional Solar Plexus:** When your mood (wave) goes down or gets low then your physical energy will go down as well.

- **Root Center connected to Spleen Center:** When the timing is right (it has to *feel* right), then you will get things done.

- **Root Center connected to your Sacral Center:** You will get things done when the formatting energies line up, as they operate in cycles of pulsing on and off.

Affirmation for your defined Root Center: "I honor my root pulse and wait for the energy to get things done. I get more done when the energy is on. When the energy is off, I know that it is my time to rest and restore myself."

If the square at the bottom of your chart is white, then you have an open Root Center. It takes in adrenaline energy from others and amplifies it.

Someone with an open Root Center might enjoy the rush of being in front of a crowd or other adrenaline-charged experiences, such as skydiving or bungee jumping. More simply, they may opt for safer adrenaline fixes, such as caffeine or chocolate.

Because this is a pressure center people can sometimes feel that they are under pressure to be free. Meaning, people who process energy this way have a hard time relaxing or playing unless all their work is done. They will feel such pressure to get things done that they don't ever allow themselves time to recharge their batteries. Eventually, they can become so drained that they are ineffective at work.

Sometimes, the energy taken in the open Root Center might be too much for a person, and they may suffer from stress or a panic disorder. People can have different levels of sensitivity in their open centers.

The truth of the open Root is that the work is never done. If you give an individual with an open Root a job to do, they will do it very quickly in order to get out from under the pressure of having to get it done.

Naturally, we tend to assign these people more work because the more work you give them, the more pressure they have to get it done, and the more they do. It can be a never-ending cycle. That's why it's crucial to realize that the open Root Center is just an energy center, and you don't have to be victim to that energy.

Question to ask yourself with an open Root Center: "Am I always in a rush to get things done so I can be free of pressure?"

Affirmation for your open Root Center: "I set realistic goals. I make powerful decisions about being free and know that things will get done when they get done. I use pressure to create more energy and at the end of the day, I rest and relax even if my to-do list is long. I make decisions according to my Human Design Strategy even if I feel pressure. I breathe and relax knowing there is an abundance of time to get things done."

• The Self-Actualization (Spleen) Center •

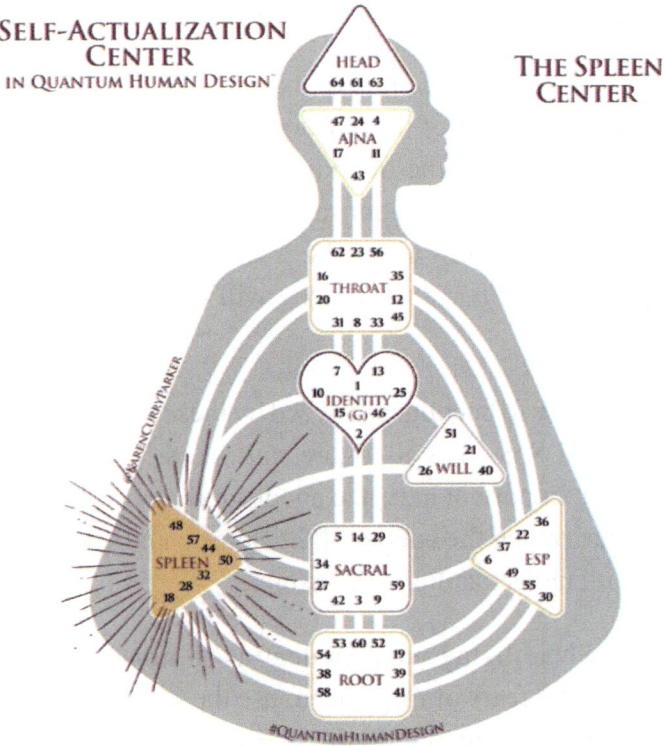

SELF-ACTUALIZATION
CENTER
IN QUANTUM HUMAN DESIGN

THE SPLEEN
CENTER

HEAD
64 61 63

47 24 4
AJNA
17   11
43

62 23 56
16   35
THROAT
20   12
31 8 33 45

7   13
1
10 IDENTITY 25
15 (G) 46
2

51
21
26 WILL 40

48
57 44
SPLEEN 50
32
28
18

5 14 29
34 SACRAL
27   59
42 3 9

36
22
37
6   ESP
49
55
30

53 60 52
54   19
38 ROOT 39
58   41

When you have a defined Spleen Center, you're designed to be in the moment. Your sense of timing will be right now. You will have a sense of time and consistent intuitive insights in the moment.

Defined Spleen Centers have very powerful immune systems. Because the immune system is so strong, it's easy for a person to miss the first symptoms of an illness. They may not notice they are sick until they are very, very sick.

It's also common for people to keep working through an illness. It's important to remember to check in with your body periodically if you have a defined Spleen. Sometimes other people may notice you are sick even before you do.

The intuition of the defined Spleen speaks *once* and then never again. That gut feeling that you should or shouldn't be doing something is your Spleen Center speaking to you.

Because the Spleen is survival based, it can also communicate to you with fear. Some of those fears include a fear of inadequacy, a fear of the future or the unknown, a fear of the past repeating itself, a fear you're failing your responsibilities, a fear of failing or that your dreams will never be realized, a fear that life is meaningless, and a fear that nothing will ever be perfect or good enough.

It's very easy to become paralyzed by these fears. The challenge of the defined Spleen is to figure out whether your intuition is giving you an important message about survival or whether you are simply experiencing the energy of the Spleen, and you need to push forward with understanding and insight.

This is where living your Strategy is so important. If you are experiencing the fears of the Spleen, use the Strategy of your Type to decide whether you should do something or not. Don't let the fears of the Spleen paralyze you into a state of inaction.

Affirmation for your defined Spleen: "I trust my intuition. I listen to my gut feelings and take guided action. I listen to my body. I rest and take care of myself. I honor my sense of time. I remember that not everyone is as fast as me and I flow with universal timing."

An open Spleen Center means that you likely have a sensitive immune system. It may seem like you get sick easily, but what that really means is that you are very sensitive to the subtle changes in your body, and you notice when you start to feel a little off. You may be very sensitive to medications, or you may even do better with homeopathic remedies.

When you have an open Spleen Center, it means that you don't have consistent access to feel-good energy. People with open Spleens like to be around people with defined Spleens. It makes them feel nurtured and strong.

People with open Spleens can have a hard time letting go. This can include possessions, addictions, relationships—even grudges.

An open center is unlimited in how it can experience the energy of that particular center. That means that you can experience unlimited intuition. It just won't always be the same. You may experience gut feelings one day, have inner knowingness on another day, and hear a guiding voice or have a prophetic dream on a different day.

Because the Spleen is also the center for time, it's common for people with open Spleens to struggle with the concept of time. Many are chronically late, while others who have had bad experiences in the past with being late are compulsively early. It can be difficult for people with open Spleens to rush.

Remember, openness is where we carry our wisdom. When a person with an open Spleen begins to understand splenic energy, they become wise about healing, intuition, and time.

Questions to ask yourself with an open Spleen Center: "Am I holding onto things (or people, pain, etc.) for longer than I should? Is fear holding me back from things I want to do in my life?"

Affirmation for your open Spleen Center: "I easily let go of all things that do not serve my highest good. I honor my body and the messages it sends me. When I feel sick, I rest. I honor my own sense of timing, respect other people's sense of time, and always wear a watch. I trust my intuition and know that I receive intuitive insights in many different ways."

• The Evolution (Sacral) Center •

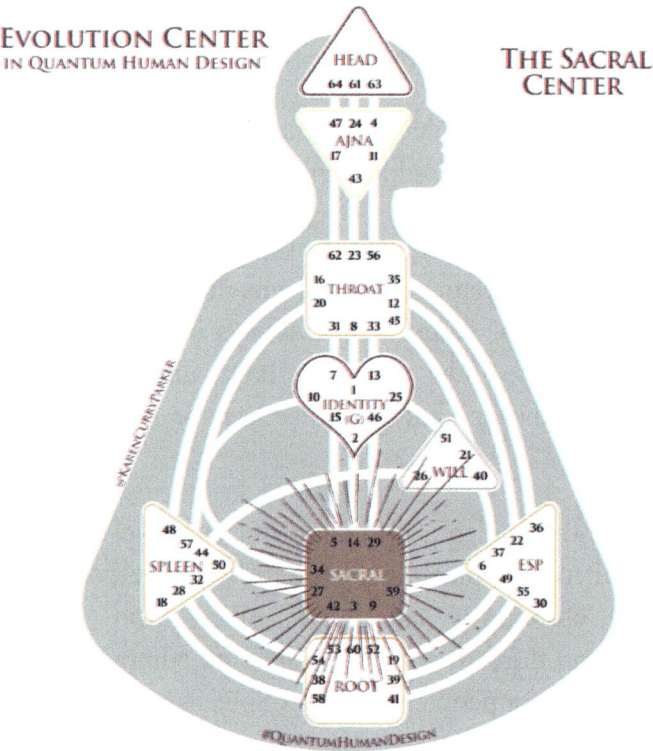

EVOLUTION CENTER
IN QUANTUM HUMAN DESIGN

THE SACRAL CENTER

When you have a defined Sacral, you are designed to work. The challenge is, of course, finding the right work that you love.

A lot of people with a defined Sacral feel frustrated because they hate their jobs and feel stuck in their work situation. This is usually because they have entered into their relationship with their work incorrectly.

The energy of the Sacral Center is counterintuitive to how most of us have been raised in this culture. Generally speaking, we have been raised to believe that we have to go out and make things happen.

If you have a defined Sacral Center, you are designed to wait for things to show up. The Sacral is all about waiting and responding to whatever shows up in your outer reality. Sacral energy works best if you learn to wait for the right thing to show up and then respond to it. Remember, though, just because it shows up doesn't mean you have to do it. You do have the freedom to choose.

Defined Sacral Centers are designed to wear themselves out every day. It's very important to sleep when you are exhausted. If you are waiting for your second wind, you are running on energy that you don't really have, and eventually your health will suffer.

If you have a defined Sacral and you are having a hard time falling asleep at night, that simply means you did not get enough physical activity during the day.

The real key to understanding Sacral energy is to understand that a defined Sacral Center gives you access to sustainable life-force and workforce energy. This is very important to remember because it is one of the key differences between a Sacral being and a non-Sacral being.

Affirmation for your defined Sacral Center: "I wait with grace and patience knowing that the right opportunities will show up for me. All I have to do is respond to the world and I will joyfully do the right work and be with the right people. I fearlessly honor my response and know that I am internally driven to be in the right place at the right time, doing the right work."

When you have an open Sacral Center, you have the ability to take in and amplify workforce and life-force energies for short periods of time.

This means that in short bursts, people with open Sacral Centers can work as hard as or even harder than those who have a defined

Sacral. But remember the key word in understanding the energy of the Sacral is sustainability and a person with an open Sacral Center cannot maintain a high level of energy for a prolonged period of time without really burning themselves out.

If you have an open Sacral Center, you are not here to work a Monday-Friday, nine-to-five job. And for most people hearing that they are not designed to work in the traditional sense is a great relief! You will probably do best finding a way to work that has some level of flexibility built into it. There are a lot of non-Sacral people who, at around forty years old, have literally fried their circuits.

Because sustainability is such an important factor in a non-Sacral being, it's important for you to always ask yourself if you are doing more than enough and to help yourself recognize when enough is enough.

Collectively, we have a lot of beliefs about the value and importance of work. A non-Sacral being does not have the energy for sustainable labor. Because of this, many non-Sacral beings get a lot of judgment from others about being lazy or incapable. But non-Sacral beings have their own wisdom and energy to add to the planet. They just work differently.

As a non-Sacral person, you need alone time to discharge the excess Sacral energy from your system. Both alone time and adequate sleep are crucial for you to stay healthy.

Question to ask yourself with an open Sacral Center: "Do I know when enough is enough?"

Affirmation for your open Sacral Center: "I am not here to work in the traditional way. I can work hard in short bursts and then I need alone time to discharge the extra energy I carry. I recognize that my energy is mutable, and I take care of myself and let go of the expectations of others. I am very powerful when I am using my energy correctly."

Channels and Gates

The nine centers on the chart are all connected to one another through what are called *channels* and they span all throughout the chart connecting to the nine centers. The channels make up the circuitry in your Design.

Each channel has a number on either end called a *gate*. There are two gates for each channel and a total of sixty-four gates. Gates represent specific energetic themes (archetypes) in our Design as human beings.

There are a total of thirty-six channels (four of the gates are used more than once in different channels). Each gate and channel in the Human Design chart has a theme or an archetype that adds a different flavor to your personality and energy configuration.

The position of the planets at the moment of our birth (and approximately three months prior to our birth) are what defines or activates the gates in our Design. The definition in our Design are energy aspects we experience consistently. Every chart has the same thirty-six channels and same sixty-four gates in the same locations. The difference between designs is what is defined (colored in) or open (white).

GATES & CHANNELS

PLANETS ACTIVATE (DEFINE) GATES

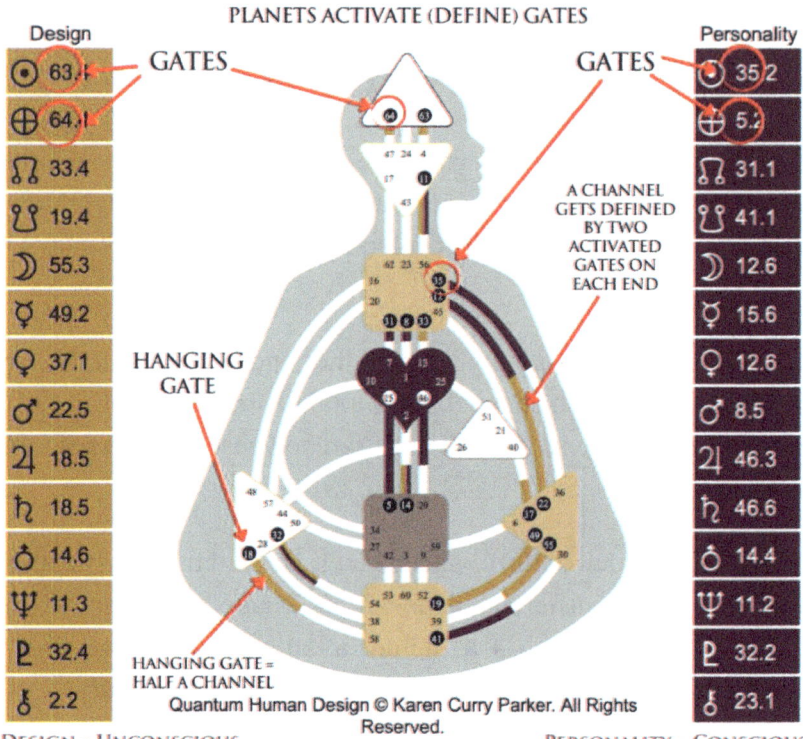

Quantum Human Design © Karen Curry Parker. All Rights Reserved.

When both gates are defined it activates the whole channel and both centers at either end of that channel.

As you can see in this picture above, Gate 12 and Gate 22 are defined along with Gate 19 and Gate 49 which defines both Channels 12/22 and 19/49. Therefore, defining the Throat, Emotional Solar Plexus and Root Centers.

When a channel is colored in **black** on traditional chart software, or deep burgundy on our chart software, that represents personality traits and energy aspects that we are consciously aware of and that is our *soul purpose*, what our soul is here to experience.

This is calculated using your birthdate or otherwise known as your conscious birthday.

When a channel is colored in *red* on traditional chart software, or gold on our chart software, that represents traits and aspects that we're not consciously aware of (our unconscious definition) and also represents the life story or life path/purpose for us in this incarnation.

The unconscious birthday is roughly three months prior to your birth and coincides with a large spurt in brain development in the cerebral cortex while a baby is in utero. It is approximately eighty-eight astrological degrees from the moment of your birth.

When a channel is colored in both black/burgundy and red/gold, it represents both the conscious and unconscious aspects and both the soul purpose and life story.

When a channel is *white* it represents an open gate at the end of it. We will always take in energy from the planets and the people around us in our openness and amplify it. We will always experience the energy in our openness in variable and inconsistent ways.

When only one of the two gates at either end of a channel is defined, it is called a *hanging gate* (like we see in the picture above with Gate 18). A person with a hanging gate, which is half a channel, is always attracted to people who have the other half of the channel. This is what we call electromagnetic attraction.

PLANETARY SYMBOLS

⊙ SUN

⊕ EARTH

♌ NORTH NODE

☋ SOUTH NODE

☽ MOON

☿ MERCURY

♀ VENUS

♂ MARS

♃ JUPITER

♄ SATURN

⚷ CHIRON

♅ URANUS

♆ NEPTUNE

♇ PLUTO

Each chart has a total of twenty-six activations designated by the thirteen planets listed on your chart *(Chiron does not activate a gate)*. The planetary positions at the moment of your birth and approximately three months *prior* to your birth are what activate or define the channels and gates in your chart. The numbers in black and the numbers in red on either side of your chart, next to the planetary symbols, correspond with the colored-in definition on your chart.

Lines, Profiles, and the Incarnation Cross

When you look at the numbers (gates) next to each planet symbol on your chart, you will see that each gate number has a smaller number next to it. For each gate there are six different *lines*, each line being a further expression of your uniqueness. The lines of the gates do not show up on the chart itself and their meaning can be revealed to you during a Human Design reading.

TRANSPERSONAL LINES ARE ENERGIES THAT ARE ALL ABOUT EXPERIENCES IN RELATIONSHIPS WITH OTHERS.

INTRAPERSONAL LINES ARE ENERGIES THAT ARE SELF-FOCUSED AND ALL ABOUT PERSONAL EXPERIENCE AND UNDERSTANDING.

@KarenCurryParker

Each line has a specific expression or personality. The position of your gates is also expressed in the lines, giving you even more insight into how that gate will be expressed in your life. Each line has a specific energy that will influence how the gate is expressed.

Lines 1 through 3 in the Profile are *intrapersonal* lines and are energies that are self-focused and all about personal experience and understanding.

Lines 4 through 6 in the Profile are about *transpersonal* energy and all about experiences in relationships with others. Some people, by Design, are focused more on their own life process, and others are more oriented toward relationships.

The 6 Lines are:

1. The Resource
2. The Responder
3. The Explorer
4. The Stabilizer
5. The Visionary Leader
6. The Adept

Line 1: The Resource

- Insatiably curious, investigative.
- Needs to *understand* before they can do anything.
- Introspective.
- Foundational line of the lower trigram.

Quantum Purpose: To lay the information foundation for the security and safety of all.

Line 2: The Responder

- Likes and needs to have alone time.
- Designed to be *called out.*
- Can be shy or coy.
- Intrapersonal/lower trigram.

Quantum Purpose: To integrate knowledge, energy, and wisdom, and wait for the readiness of others to call them out.

Line 3: The Explorer

- Learns what works by first learning what doesn't work.
- Here to be experts in what works based on experience.
- No such things as a mistake or failure if a lesson was learned.
- Experiential learners.
- Intrapersonal/lower trigram.

Quantum Purpose: To explore and experience possibilities and share your experiences with others to protect and serve them.

Line 4: The Stabilizer

- Foundation of the upper trigram.
- Transpersonal.
- Moves from one foundation to the next.
- Fixed.
- Uncomfortable with limbo or uncertainty.
- Their relationships and connections are everything to them.
- They care deeply and are highly sensitive to judgment and criticism.

Quantum Purpose: To lay the foundation of community and connection and prepare the way for sharing and spreading of ideas.

Line 5: The Visionary Leader

- Universalizes whatever is in their chart.
- "Savior" or not depending on the projection field.
- Mysterious, seductive, compelling, persuasive.
- Transpersonal.

Quantum Purpose: To serve as a Karmic Mirror for others and to support the healing process through reflection by teaching and sharing the highest potential of humanity possible.

Line 6: The Adept

- Triphasic life cycle.
  * Phase 1 - age 0-29: Pioneering phase-exploring and experimentation.
  * Phase 2 - age 30-49: "On the Roof" learning and healing through integration, introspection, and reflection.
  * Phase 3 - age 50-end of life: Chiron Return - Fully adept and embodied, to share what they're here to share with the world as a role model.
- Can seem aloof.
- Late bloomers.
- Transpersonal.

Quantum Purpose: To experience, integrate and demonstrate the highest potential of consciousness on the planet and to quietly show us how to live it.

There are twelve different personality Profiles in Human Design. A Profile comes from the lines of the gates in a chart's conscious and unconscious Sun sign. The Sun sign is the first sign on a chart under the **Soul Purpose** and **Life Story** columns, also known as Mind/Body or Personality/Design**.**

The lines are the little numbers just to the right of the big numbers. They look like exponents (or a number being raised "to the power of" in mathematics).

Profiles tell you about major life themes that you will encounter, and they illustrate another way in which your personality interacts with the world. Everyone comes into the world with a specific Profile and purpose. Knowing your Profile can help you see some of the themes that you will encounter as you move toward fulfilling your purpose.

Your Profile shows you the character you're here to play in this incarnation.

Each number in a Profile has a specific meaning. The first number in your Profile is an element of your personality that you will be **consciously** aware of. The second number in the Profile may be **unconscious** and more hidden from you.

PROFILE = CHARACTER YOU'RE HERE TO PLAY

2/4 - Conscious & Unconscious Sun Lines = Your Profile (Character)

There are a total of 12 Profiles

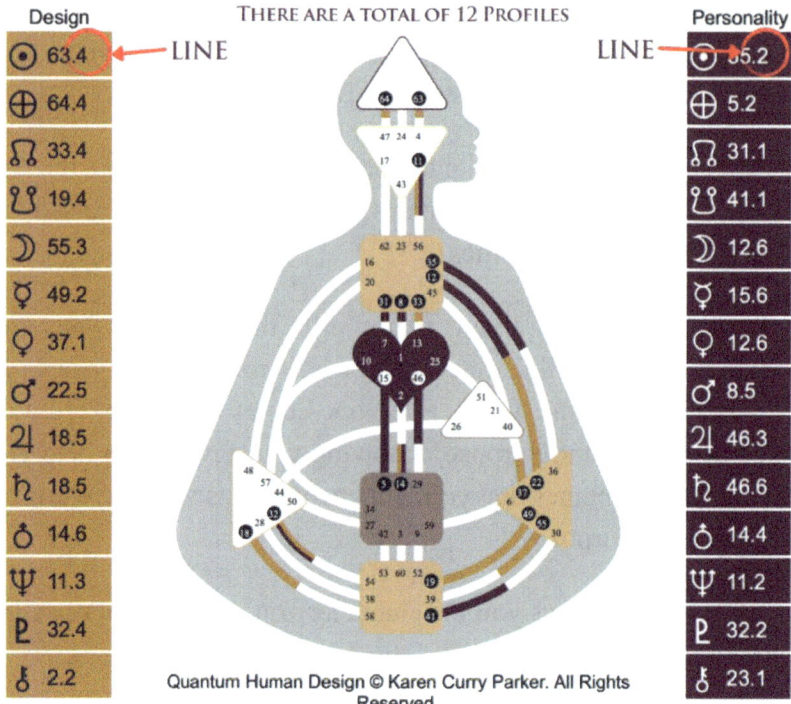

Design		Personality	
⊙	63.4	⊙	35.2
⊕	64.4	⊕	5.2
☊	33.4	☊	31.1
☋	19.4	☋	41.1
☽	55.3	☽	12.6
☿	49.2	☿	15.6
♀	37.1	♀	12.6
♂	22.5	♂	8.5
♃	18.5	♃	46.3
♄	18.5	♄	46.6
♅	14.6	♅	14.4
♆	11.3	♆	11.2
♇	32.4	♇	32.2
☊	2.2	☊	23.1

LINE ← (Design 63.4)   LINE ← (Personality 35.2)

The twelve Profiles are derived from the six possible lines of a particular gate. Each of these six lines represents a different archetype or style of behavior.

Your Profile can be thought of as an explanation of your conscious and unconscious archetype and the themes associated with that archetype. Most people are aware of their unconscious Profile but because it is unconscious, they do not have a lot of real control over the expression of it.

The **twelve Profiles** are combinations of two gate lines (the **conscious** line followed by the **unconscious** line):

- 1/3 Resource/Explorer
- 1/4 Resource/Stabilizer
- 2/4 Responder/Stabilizer
- 2/5 Responder/Visionary Leader
- 3/5 Explorer/Visionary Leader
- 3/6 Explorer/Adept
- 4/6 Stabilizer/Adept
- 4/1 Stabilizer/Resource
- 5/1 Visionary Leader/Resource
- 5/2 Visionary Leader/Responder
- 6/2 Adept/Responder
- 6/3 Adept/Explorer

The final piece of the chart that ties the whole thing together is called the *Incarnation Cross*. The Incarnation Cross is comprised of the energies that make up your conscious and unconscious Sun and Earth signs—the top four black and red numbers on your Human Design chart.

These four energies combined comprise about 70 percent of your personality expression. The Incarnation Cross is basically the storyline that a person is here to play and live out.

HUMAN DESIGN CHART

INCARNATION CROSS 29/30 | 8/14

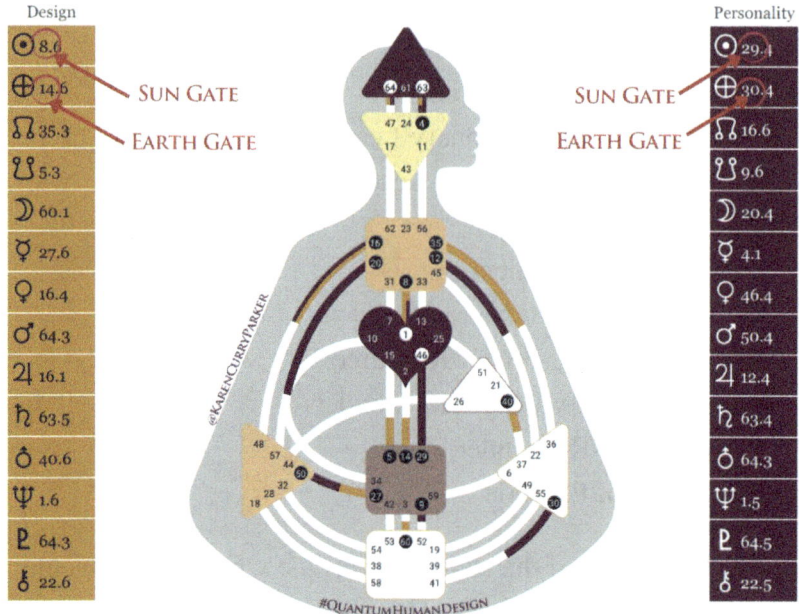

Quantum Human Design © Karen Curry Parker. All Rights Reserved.

There are a total of 192 basic Incarnation Crosses, each one a reflection of the Solar and Earth transits and each basic cross has multiple variations for each, making up over 700 crosses. The Incarnation Cross offers us a deeper explanation of the path of a soul and the journey of a lifetime.

If you would like more information on Incarnation Crosses, please visit:
https://learn.quantumhumandesign.com/products/intro-to-qhd

Definition

The *definition* of the chart refers to the colored-in channels or connections between centers.

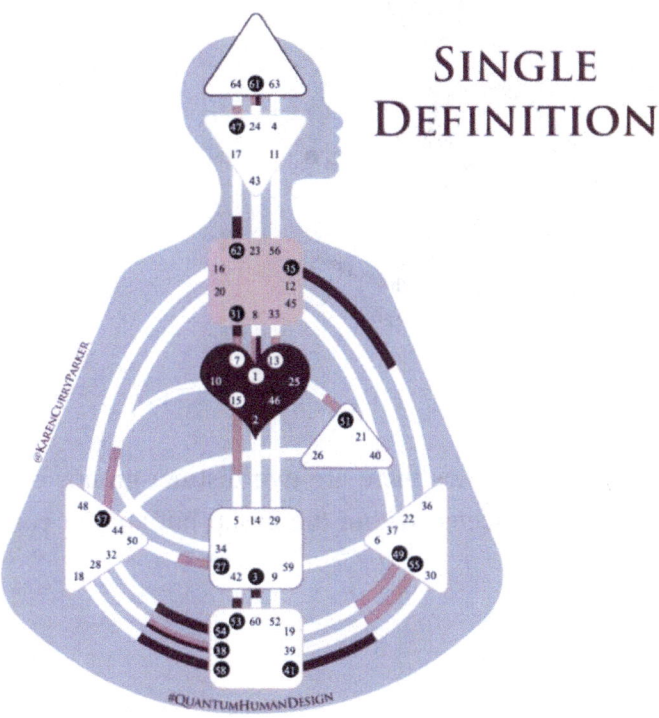

Single definition means all of the centers that are colored in or defined in the chart are connected.

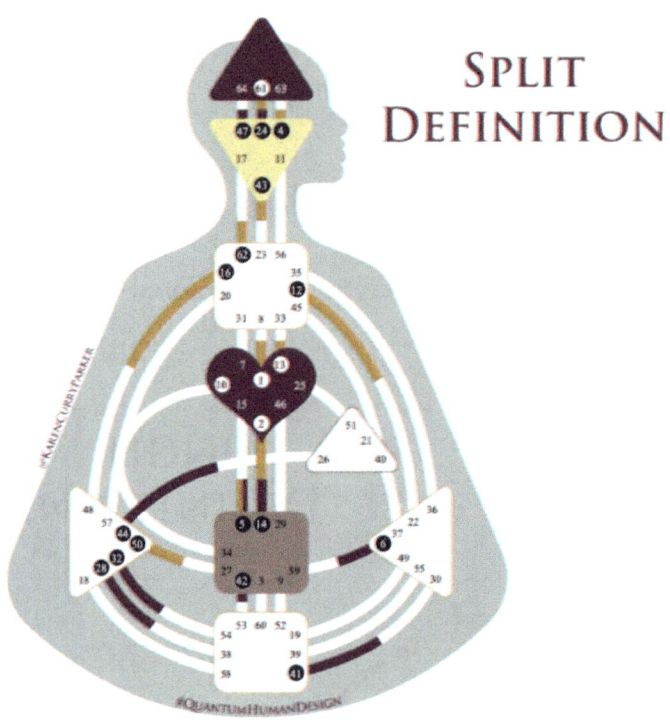

Split definition means there are two distinct groups of energy centers that are connected within the group but are not connected to each other.

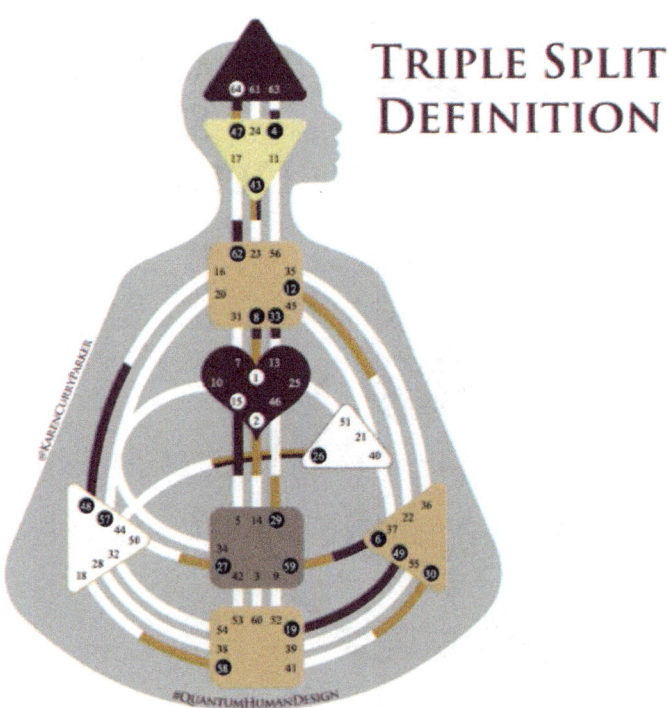

Triple Split definition means there are three distinct groupings of energy centers that are independent and not connected to one another.

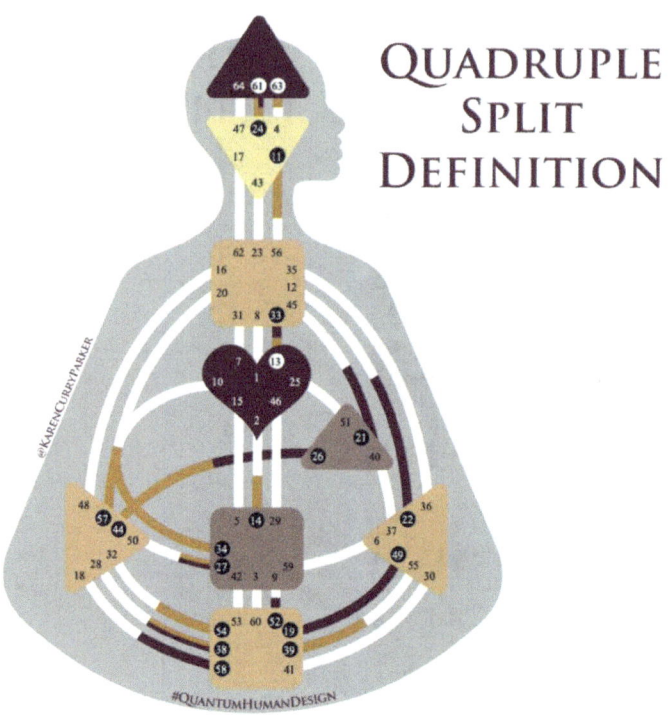

QUADRUPLE
SPLIT
DEFINITION

Quadruple Split definition means there are four distinct groupings of energy centers that are independent and not connected to one another. Quadruple Split definition is fairly rare.

An energy split can make you feel as if you have certain very distinct aspects to your perception of yourself. For example, in this chart (see above), you may feel you have a very powerful mind and can get lost in your head but that you also have an "earthy" and primal part of your personality as well.

We are often attracted to partners who have the gates that "bridge" our defined splits. When we are with that person, we feel whole or that all the parts of ourselves are unified, which is indeed what happens, at least energetically.

ELECTROMAGNETIC GATES

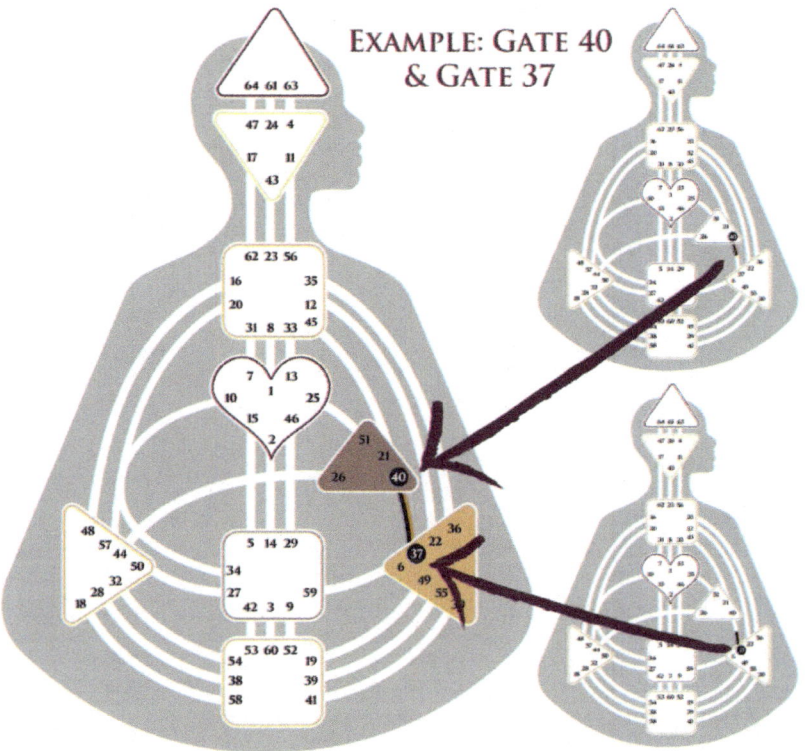

EXAMPLE: GATE 40
& GATE 37

Conclusion

When we are born, the energy of the world begins to take us away from the truth of who we really are. Your genetic lineage, your experiences, your pain, your trauma, and the beliefs that you learn from the people around you, condition you away from that truth.

The Universe is infinitely wise and kind. Despite how we might struggle and even turn away from the truth of who we really are, the Universe continues to leave us clues all along the way.

Living true to your Human Design Type allows you to interface and connect with the natural abundance of the ***cosmic plan*** and supports you in aligning with your destiny—the lessons you sought to learn and overcome before you even incarnated.

It seems counterintuitive sometimes that living true to ourselves simply means following what feels right and good in a way that *feels* right and good. We do have to struggle to grow at times. Struggle is in our hardwiring…*Suffering is not.*

We suffer when we turn away from ourselves. We suffer when we resist who we truly are. Resistance to our authentic self is the greatest source of pain in people's lives.

You owe it to yourself to live in a way that is true to who you really are.

You also owe it to the world.

Imagine for a moment that every human being on the planet represents a colorful thread that, when woven together, makes a beautiful tapestry. The tapestry is only as beautiful as the sum of all the threads. If a thread is out of place, missing, or pulled, it affects the entire face of the tapestry.

You play an important part in this world. You are so important that we would not be who we are right now without you.

At this crucial junction in time, the world needs you to take your right place—the place you intended for yourself to take before you even incarnated.

Living true to your Human Design Type and Strategy, allows you to follow the path you set out for yourself, minimize pain and resistance and, ultimately, step into the full and easy expression of *who you truly are*.

From my heart to yours,
Karen Curry Parker

About the Author

Karen Curry Parker is a transformational teacher, speaker, and coach. She is a multiple bestselling author, EFT (Emotional Freedom Techniques) practitioner since 2000, life coach since 1998, an original student of Ra Uru Hu, and one of the world's leading Human Design teachers since 1999. She is also a Quantum University PhD student and guest lecturer, and a TEDx presenter.

Karen is the founder and creator of two certification trainings: The Quantum Human Design for Everyone Training System™ and The Quantum Alignment System™. She is also the founder of the Understanding Human Design Community. She is the host of the Quantum rEvolution and Cosmic Revolution podcasts and co-founder of GracePoint Publishing.

Karen has a deep love for helping people activate their highest potential, which in part is why she created Quantum Human Design™. Her core mission is to help people live the life they were designed to live by discovering who they are, what they are here to do, and how to activate their authentic life path by waking them up to the power of their innate creativity and unlimited possibility.

Karen is a 4/6 Time Bender (Manifesting Generator), mother of eight amazing humans, wife of a genius, and grandmother of two emerging world leaders. She has her BSN in nursing, a BA in journalism, and is currently working on her PhD in integrative health at Quantum University.

Ways You Can Stay Connected

Join the Understanding Human Design online community
@KarenCurryParker

Enroll in courses.
KarenCurryParker.Teachable.com

Join the community.
KarenCurryParker.Circle.so

Want to become a certified Quantum Human Design specialist?
Enroll in professional training here:
QuantumAlignmentSystem.com/ProTraining

For more great books from Human Design Press
Visit Books.GracePointPublishing.com

If you enjoyed reading Introduction of Quantum Human Design, and purchased
it through an online retailer, please return to the site and write a review to help
others find the book.